# RECIPES FOR THE
# LOAF PAN

**Rose Grant**

**BRISTOL PUBLISHING ENTERPRISES**
San Leandro, California

# A Nitty Gritty® Cookbook

Printed in the United States of America.

ISBN 1-55867-137-4

Cover design: Frank J. Paredes
Cover photography: John A. Benson
Food stylist: Suzanne Carreiro
Illustrator: James Balkovek
Indexer: Rose Grant

# CONTENTS

To our grandsons, who have enriched our lives
beyond our fondest expectations.
In order of their appearance:
Daniel, Jefferson, Michael, Nile, Aaron,
Reed, and the little person, as yet unknown.
Also, to Neva, the one with the red pen.
And, of course, to my husband Philip,
who gives us all a reason to celebrate.

# ABOUT LOAF PANS AND LOAVES

**"We know that bread is the staff of life — but that is
no reason for the life of the staff to be one long loaf."**
**(sign seen in a British bake shop)**

## ABOUT THE PANS

The versatile loaf pan is small and nonthreatening. Unlike the battery of pots and pans designed for just one purpose, the simple loaf pan can be used in many ways. If you have a small kitchen, limited funds or not much time to create elaborate meals, a skillet and a couple of loaf pans can satisfy most of your culinary needs. It is truly a pan for all reasons.

There is a wide variety of loaf pans from which to choose. The ordinary aluminium or glass loaf pan does a fine job. With a few notable exceptions, I'd have to say that, if given a test, I could not tell the difference in the end product whether I used an inexpensive metal pan, a glass pan, a clay pan or a top-of-the-line nonstick steel pan. Most recipes can be prepared in the simplest of pans.

But there are intangible differences between pans, just as there are between knives. All knives can cut food, but a heavy, well-balanced knife that fits into your hand soon becomes a kitchen friend. Pans, too, can become friends. It is easy to develop a special relationship with a **professional quality steel pan with nonstick coating**. Heavy and well-crafted, with no sharp edges, it feels great in the hand and invites frequent use.

**Glass and porcelain loaf pans** have always been used for meat loaves and desserts, especially if they are to be brought to the table. Of course, any glass pan that goes into a hot oven should be made of ovenware glass. Many of them are decorative and some have **a fitted plastic top**, which makes them perfect for the portable feast. Glass and porcelain are also suitable for the microwave oven and the freezer.

If you have never used a **clay or earthenware loaf pan**, you should treat yourself to one, especially if you bake bread. The pan should be porous, unglazed and free from harmful chemicals. Terra cotta pans are gentle to live yeast, allowing it to "breathe." As a result, a bread baked in an earthenware pan will rise as much as one inch higher than an identical loaf baked in a metal pan. A clay pan makes a higher, crisper crust.

There are also **miniature loaf pans**, both clay and metal. At first, I couldn't figure why I should use a pan that holds a cup or two of batter. "Obviously, you do not have a child in school," I was told. A small bread given in a little pan makes a fine teacher's gift. Many of the fruitcake and tea bread recipes will fit into 3 or 4 small pans, for giving or freezing. Put a small quantity of meat loaf or vegetable loaf in a miniature pan, and bake it along with the larger loaf (be sure to take it out of the oven before the large loaf is done; it does not need as much time). It makes a great lunch.

A fairly recent, welcome addition to the loaf pan collection is the **pan with a drip rack** that allows fat to drain through holes as the loaf bakes. One version is actually a two-pan system, one slightly smaller pan fitting into a larger pan. Since both pans have a nonstick surface, cleanup takes next to no time. A less expensive version of the two-pan loaf pan is a single pan with a flat, slotted metal trivet, which also drains the fat away from the loaf. If you do not have either pan, be sure to drain the fat from the meat loaf as soon as it is removed from the oven; simply tip the pan and drain the fat into a container to be discarded.

## ABOUT THE RECIPES

### Simplicity

Many recipes can be prepared in one bowl. Where the instructions say, "Combine all ingredients," it doesn't make much difference in what order the ingredients are added. Unless the instructions say to use an electric mixer, a wooden spoon does as well.

Ease of preparation has also been considered. This is a book to be used every day, when time and effort count. You can prepare smaller quantities than in a regular casserole dish and can serve directly from the pan. Leftovers stay in the pan to be reheated for a second go-round. The loaf pan, being an unpretentious utensil, lends itself to everyday cooking. It is especially useful for a small family.

## Storing the end result

Practically all of the recipes in this book can be doubled. That means one loaf for now and one for later. In general, any loaf can be kept in the refrigerator for a week. Most loaves can be frozen, whether or not the recipe says so. Quick breads freeze very well. Since it takes very little extra effort to make an extra bread, preparing two breads rather than one is good use of time. Be sure to store breads in a heavy, freezer-weight plastic bag. Yeasted breads usually freeze, with only minor loss of quality, for about 3 weeks.

## About the ingredients

Most of the recipes in this book have been "slenderized" to accommodate today's healthier eating habits. In only two cases is sour cream used without the suggestion that unflavored yogurt can be substituted. Many of the recipes that called for ground beef 15 years ago now call for ground turkey. The number of eggs has been cut. In many recipes, cream has been replaced with milk.

I use very little canned or frozen food. I do not have a sense of mission about fresh food only, but I do think it is better — and since fresh products are readily available, I continue to use them. With few exceptions, notably spinach and beans, I prefer to substitute one fresh vegetable for another rather than use canned or frozen foods. Zucchini can become broccoli; green beans can substitute for peas.

## Unmolding loaves

Most breads unmold without protest; just turn the bread over onto a rack. The same is true for meat loaves, especially if you use a nonstick pan. For other loaves, a towel soaked in hot water, wrung dry and placed on the bottom of the loaf pan can often coax a stubborn loaf to drop onto the platter.

## Servings

My very general rule is that a meat or vegetable loaf will nourish 4 to 6 people of varying appetites. Bread loaves and desserts will yield 10 to 12 servings.

# POULTRY AND SEAFOOD LOAVES

# CHICKEN WITH ARTICHOKES

*The flavor of the marinated artichokes enhances the flavor of the chicken and makes this loaf somewhat special. Add Italian herbs for a little more zing.*

2 jars (6 oz. each) marinated artichoke
  hearts, drained, liquid reserved
1 tbs. butter or margarine, melted
1 medium onion, chopped
1 lb. chicken breasts and thighs,
  skinned and boned

½ cup Italian-seasoned breadcrumbs
1 tsp. dried tarragon
1 tsp. dried dill
salt and pepper to taste
1 egg, lightly beaten
½ cup whole milk or half-and-half

Preheat oven to 350°. Grease an 8-x-4-inch loaf pan, glass if possible. In a food processor bowl, place artichoke liquid, butter, onion, chicken, breadcrumbs and seasonings; process until coarsely chopped. Remove contents to a large bowl. Add egg and milk to processor bowl and process for a few seconds, just enough to incorporate leftover chicken mixture with egg and milk. Add to bowl and mix well.

Cut artichoke hearts into small pieces and add to loaf mixture. Mix well. Transfer mixture to prepared loaf pan. Place loaf pan in a larger baking pan. Add enough hot water to come halfway up sides of loaf pan. Bake for 1 hour or until top is brown and loaf is firm. Remove from oven and cool in pan for 10 minutes. Drain off any liquid and turn out loaf onto an oval platter.

# CHICKEN LOAF WITH MUSHROOM SAUCE

*Fresh "wild" mushrooms take this loaf out of the ordinary (these mushrooms are raised for commercial sale; please don't take to the woods in search of mushrooms unless you know what you're doing). Served with mushroom sauce, it makes an elegant presentation.*

3 cups chicken stock (prefer homemade)
2 cups cubed day-old Italian or French bread
4 cups coarsely chopped cooked chicken
2 cups cooked brown rice (1 cup can be cooked wild rice)
4 eggs, beaten

¾ cup chopped green or red bell pepper (or combination)
salt and pepper to taste
1 tbs. fresh minced sage, or 1 tsp. dried
1 tsp. dried rosemary
1 small onion, finely chopped
*Mushroom Sauce*, follows

Preheat oven to 350°. Generously butter a heavy-weight loaf pan. In a large bowl, pour chicken stock over bread and toss; allow to stand until stock has been absorbed. Combine bread with chicken, rice and all other loaf ingredients. Mix well. Spoon into prepared loaf pan. Place loaf pan in a larger baking pan. Add enough hot water to come halfway up sides of loaf pan. Bake for 1 hour. Cool for 30 minutes and invert onto a platter. Serve with *Mushroom Sauce.*

## MUSHROOM SAUCE

2 tbs. butter
1 small onion, finely chopped
1½ cups coarsely chopped mushrooms
    (prefer portobello or shiitake)
¼ cup butter
¼ cup flour (or more)

2½ cups chicken stock
2 tbs. chopped fresh parsley
1 tbs. lemon juice
salt and white pepper to taste
½ tsp. paprika

Melt 2 tbs. butter in a small skillet. Add chopped onion and mushrooms; sauté over low heat until mushrooms have softened. Remove from heat and set aside.

Melt ¼ cup butter in a small saucepan over low heat. Gradually add flour, stirring until smooth. Cook for 1 minute, stirring constantly. Stir in stock a little at a time (to prevent lumps). Cook over medium heat until sauce is thick and bubbly. Add onion-mushroom mixture, parsley, lemon juice and seasonings. Keep warm until ready to serve.

# CHICKEN STUFFING WITH FRUIT

*Serve this extra stuffing in a clay loaf pan, if you have one. It keeps the stuffing warm and moist. The stuffing can be baked alongside a roasting chicken.*

1 loaf day-old Italian or French bread, cut into
    small cubes (about 6 cups)
1 cup minced celery
½ cup minced carrot
1 apple, peeled and coarsely chopped
    (prefer Granny Smith)
2 tsp. minced fresh sage, or ½ tsp. dried
2 tsp. minced fresh thyme, or ½ tsp. dried
½ tsp. allspice
½ cup chopped mixed dried fruit, or choose 1 or 2
¼ cup white wine
¼ cup water

Preheat oven to 350°. Lightly grease a loaf pan. In a large bowl, combine all dry ingredients. Combine wine and water and add to bread mixture until just moistened; it should not be mushy. Bake for 40 minutes until crusty on top. If it gets too brown, cover with aluminum foil after 30 minutes.

# TURKEY LOAF OLÉ

*Serve this with tortilla chips and a tomato salad.*

1 lb. ground turkey
1 cup chopped onion
2 cloves garlic, chopped
½ cup chopped green or red bell pepper
1 can (16 oz.) kidney beans, rinsed and
  drained
1 can (8 oz.) tomato sauce
1 can (4 oz.) diced green chiles, drained

1 tbs. chili powder, or to taste
1 tsp. dried oregano leaves or dried
  mixed Italian herbs
1 tsp. ground cumin, optional
1 cup water
½ cup cornmeal
1 cup shredded cheddar cheese
chopped fresh cilantro, optional

Preheat oven to 375°. Combine ground turkey with onion, garlic, pepper, kidney beans, tomato sauce, chiles and seasonings, except chopped cilantro. Mix well. Place in a 9-x-5-inch loaf pan.

In a small saucepan, bring water to a boil. Add cornmeal slowly (to prevent lumps) and cook, stirring constantly, for about 2 minutes until thick. Stir cheese into hot mixture. Spread evenly over turkey mixture. Bake for about 30 minutes until top is brown. Let stand for about 5 minutes before serving. Top with chopped cilantro.

# TURKEY-SPINACH LOAF

*The pesto sauce is the key ingredient in this moist, tasty loaf. Homemade pesto sauce is preferred, but you can use the pesto sauce found in the refrigerator case in the supermarket, near the fresh pasta. It's important to squeeze the spinach until it is very dry.*

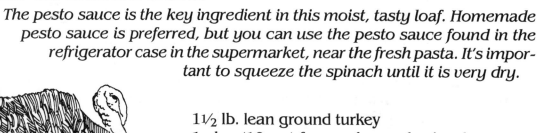

1½ lb. lean ground turkey
1 pkg. (10 oz.) frozen chopped spinach,
    thawed and squeezed dry
⅓ cup quick-cooking rolled oats (not instant)
2 tbs. oat bran
¼ cup pesto sauce
2 tbs. water
salt and pepper to taste

Preheat oven to 350°. In a bowl, combine all ingredients. Pack into a nonstick loaf pan. Bake for about 1 hour.

# TURKEY LOAF WITH GUACAMOLE

*This easy-to-prepare loaf is served on a bed of guacamole for an attractive presentation. You can vary the spiciness of this dish, according to taste.*

## GUACAMOLE

1 ripe avocado
1 small ripe tomato, chopped

2 tbs. lemon juice
1 tbs. chopped fresh cilantro

Mash avocado in a small bowl. Stir in remaining ingredients. Set aside.

1 lb. lean ground turkey
1 cup shredded Monterey Jack cheese
   (can be peppered or with pimiento)
¾ cup seasoned breadcrumbs
1 can (4 oz.) chopped green chiles, mild
   or hot, drained

1 egg, lightly beaten
½ cup salsa, mild or hot
½ tsp. dried oregano
½ tsp. ground cumin
salt and pepper to taste
chopped fresh cilantro for garnish

Preheat oven to 375°. Grease a loaf pan. Combine all loaf ingredients in a bowl. Mix well, and transfer into loaf pan. Bake for about 1 hour. Let stand in pan for about 10 minutes. Unmold turkey loaf on a bed of guacamole. Sprinkle with chopped cilantro.

# TURKEY MEAT LOAF WITH MUSHROOM-TOMATO SAUCE

*A clay pan makes a very moist loaf. If you use a pan with a trivet, it will be a little drier, since much of the fat will drip through the holes. This loaf is company fare. Serve it with rice and a green vegetable or salad.*

1½ lb. lean ground turkey breast
2 cups seasoned breadcrumbs
1 cup finely chopped green onions
1 small yellow onion, chopped
½ cup coarsely chopped mushrooms (prefer portobello)
2 cloves garlic, finely chopped
1 tbs. peeled, chopped ginger root (or less)
½ cup chicken stock (or a little more)
1 egg
1 egg white
salt and pepper to taste
*Mushroom-Tomato Sauce*, follows

Preheat oven to 350°. Lightly grease a 9-x-5-inch loaf pan. In a large bowl, combine all ingredients for turkey loaf, except sauce. Place in prepared loaf pan. Cover loaf tightly with aluminum foil. Bake for 1¼ hours. Set loaf aside, still covered, while you prepare *Mushroom-Tomato Sauce*. To serve, remove foil and plastic wrap. Unmold loaf and top with sauce.

## MUSHROOM-TOMATO SAUCE

1 tbs. olive oil
1 small onion, thinly sliced
1 large stalk celery, chopped
1 tbs. chopped garlic
1½ cups thinly sliced mushrooms

1 can (1 lb.) crushed tomatoes
1 tsp. dried mixed Italian herbs (or less)
   or Herbes de Provence
1 tsp. sugar
salt and pepper to taste

Place olive oil in a large skillet. Sauté onion, celery, garlic and mushrooms until vegetables are limp. Add tomatoes and seasonings and cook for about 10 minutes over low heat.

# TURKEY STUFFING

*If your turkey never seems to have enough stuffing, this recipe makes a wonderful addition to a holiday table. You could use one kind of stuffing for the turkey and another kind for extras. Use a clay pan, if possible; it makes moist, delicious stuffing and keeps the heat very well.*

½ lb. sweet sausage, (or more) casing
   removed
2 tbs. butter
1 cup finely chopped onion
2 cloves garlic, finely chopped
1 cup finely chopped celery
2 cups stale bread cubes, about 1-inch
2 cups coarsely crumbled cornbread

½ cup apple juice or apple cider
2 tbs. butter, melted
1 egg, lightly beaten
1 tsp. dried basil
1 tsp. dried thyme
½ tsp. dried sage
salt and pepper to taste

Preheat oven to 350°. Lightly grease a loaf pan. Chop sausage coarsely and sauté in a medium skillet for 10 minutes over low heat. Discard fat. In same skillet, melt butter. Add onion, garlic and celery and cook until softened. In a large bowl, combine sausage-onion mixture with remaining ingredients. Add a little more apple juice if mixture seems dry. Transfer to loaf pan and bake for about 40 to 50 minutes. Serve from loaf pan.

# TURKEY PIZZA LOAF

*You can change the character of this meat loaf by substituting lean ground beef for the ground turkey. Or use pork sausage instead of turkey sausage. These "wild" mushrooms are raised for commercial sale; don't go into the woods for mushrooms.*

1 lb. turkey sausage
1 lb. lean ground turkey
¾ cup Italian-seasoned breadcrumbs
1 tsp. fennel seed (or less)
2 tsp. dried mixed Italian herbs (or less)
½ lb. portobello (or other wild) mushrooms
1 medium onion, chopped

2 cloves garlic, finely chopped
2 eggs, lightly beaten
1 red or green bell pepper, chopped
salt and white pepper to taste
½ jar (14 oz.) pizza or spaghetti sauce
1 can (4 oz.) chopped black olives, drained

**TOPPING**
½ jar (14 oz.) pizza or spaghetti sauce
2 cans (4 oz. each) sliced black olives, drained

Preheat oven to 350°. In a large bowl, combine all meat loaf ingredients. Mix well. Place in a nonstick loaf pan with a trivet to drain off most of the fat. Bake for 1 hour or more, until done. After 45 minutes, top loaf with ½ jar pizza sauce and olives, and continue baking for another 15 to 20 minutes. Let stand for about 10 minutes before slicing.

# SEAFOOD MUSHROOM BAKE

*You can change the proportions, add to or subtract any of the seafood, or change the mushrooms to drained marinated artichoke hearts. No matter what you do to this recipe, it seems to improve.*

3 tbs. butter
1/2 lb. mushrooms (cremini, if possible)
1 onion, chopped
2 cloves garlic, finely minced
3 tbs. butter
3 tbs. flour
1 1/2 cups milk
1/2 cup dry white wine (prefer Chablis)
salt and pepper to taste
1 tsp. dried tarragon
2 tbs. minced fresh parsley (prefer flat-leaf Italian-style)

1/2 lb. uncooked shrimp, peeled and deveined
1/2 lb. cooked lobster meat
1/2 lb. cooked fresh crabmeat
1/2 lb. uncooked bay scallops
1/2 cup grated imported Parmesan cheese
1/2 cup breadcrumbs
1/2 tsp. paprika
fresh parsley for garnish

Preheat oven 350°. Lightly grease a nonstick 9-x-5-inch loaf pan. In a medium skillet, melt 3 tbs. butter. Add mushrooms, onion and garlic. Sauté until vegetables become limp, about 5 minutes. In a large skillet, melt 3 tbs. butter, add flour and stir until thick. Add milk, a little at a time, and stir until smooth. Add wine, salt, pepper, tarragon and parsley. Stir until thick and very smooth. Remove from heat. Add mushroom mixture and seafood to cream sauce and mix well. Adjust seasonings.

Place in loaf pan. Combine Parmesan cheese with breadcrumbs and sprinkle on top of loaf. Sprinkle with paprika. Bake for about 45 minutes, until shrimp have turned pink. Do not overbake. Garnish with additional parsley.

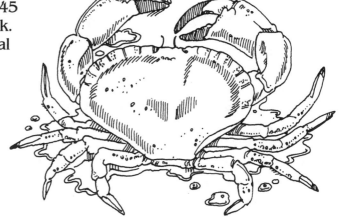

# SHRIMP AND RICE CREOLE

*This is a simple dish to prepare. Filé powder can be found among the spices in your supermarket. You can add leftover ham or chicken or any cooked vegetable that needs eating. A clay pan makes an attractive presentation.*

2 tbs. vegetable oil
1 onion, chopped
1 red or green bell pepper, chopped
1 large clove garlic, finely minced
2 cups canned whole Italian tomatoes
1 cup dry white wine
1 tsp. filé powder (or more)

1 tsp. (or more) ground cumin
salt and pepper to taste
1 lb. shrimp, peeled and deveined
2-3 cups cold cooked rice
1 cup dried breadcrumbs
3 tbs. butter, melted
2 tbs. chopped fresh cilantro for garnish

Preheat oven to 375°. In a large skillet, heat oil and sauté onion, pepper and garlic until vegetables are limp, about 5 minutes. Stir in tomatoes, wine, filé powder, cumin, salt and pepper. Simmer for about 10 minutes, stirring occasionally. Add shrimp. Cook just until shrimp turn pink, about 3 minutes. Add cooked rice and stir to coat.

Toss breadcrumbs with melted butter. Set aside. Place shrimp-rice mixture in a 9-x-5-inch loaf pan. Top with breadcrumbs and bake until bubbly, about 30 minutes. Top with chopped cilantro.

# SALMON LOAF

*When salmon was inexpensive and plentiful, every cook had a recipe for this trusty standby. Now that it is a luxury, you don't see salmon loaf nearly as often. This recipe is absolutely wonderful with fresh salmon, but a 1-pound can of salmon (skin and bones removed and well-drained) works almost as well. Of course, you can use tuna, both fresh and canned, in place of the salmon. You can serve this with a hollandaise sauce, but it really isn't necessary.*

2 tbs. butter
½ cup chopped green onions
1½ cups soft breadcrumbs
½ cup mayonnaise
¼ cup sour cream
1 tsp. Dijon mustard (or more)
1 tbs. bottled chili sauce, optional
2 tbs. fresh lemon juice (or more)

2 tbs. chopped fresh dill weed
2 tbs. chopped fresh parsley
1 egg, lightly beaten
salt and pepper to taste
1 lb. cooked salmon, in chunks, skin
    and bones removed
fresh dill weed for garnish

Preheat oven to 350°. Lightly grease a glass loaf pan or a nonstick pan. Combine all ingredients, except salmon. Mix well. Add salmon and mix carefully so that salmon remains in chunks. Turn into prepared loaf pan and bake until loaf is set in the center, about 50 to 60 minutes. Cool on a wire rack for about 10 minutes. Garnish.

# TUNA-BROCCOLI SOUFFLÉ

*This loaf won't wait for several hours. As with any soufflé, it begins to sink soon after it comes out of the oven. Plan to serve it immediately.*

cornmeal for sprinkling
2 cups milk
½ cup cornmeal
2 tbs. butter or margarine
½ cup thinly sliced green onions
1 lb. broccoli, trimmed and coarsely
   chopped

1 can (6 oz.) water-packed tuna,
   drained and flaked
salt and pepper to taste
1 tsp. dried dill weed
1 cup shredded sharp cheddar cheese
2 eggs, separated

Preheat oven to 400°. Grease a glass 9-x-5-inch loaf pan and sprinkle with cornmeal. In a large saucepan over high heat, bring milk to a boil; slowly sprinkle in cornmeal, stirring constantly. Lower heat and cook until thickened, about 3 minutes, stirring occasionally; remove from heat. Melt butter in a medium skillet. Sauté broccoli and green onions for 5 minutes. Stir broccoli and onions into cornmeal with tuna, seasonings and cheddar cheese. Blend in egg yolks. Mix well.

In a small bowl, beat egg whites until stiff peaks form; gently fold into broccoli mixture. Spoon into prepared loaf pan. Bake for 30 minutes or until puffed and golden. Serve immediately.

# MEAT LOAVES

# CARROT MEAT LOAF

*This loaf combines meat and carrots for a very satisfying main dish. It's easy to fix; it's tasty; it's low in calories. Bake in a loaf pan with a trivet, if you're concerned about cholesterol; most of the fat will drain through the holes.*

1 lb. lean ground beef
1 cup shredded carrots
1 medium onion, chopped
1 clove garlic, chopped
¾ cup crushed cornflakes
1 cup skim milk
1 egg, lightly beaten
salt and pepper to taste
1 tbs. Worcestershire sauce
1 tsp. ground cumin, optional
2 tbs. chopped fresh cilantro, optional

Preheat oven to 350°. In a large bowl, combine all ingredients. Mix until just blended; do not overmix. Place in a 9-x-5-inch nonstick loaf pan. Bake for about 50 minutes. Serve hot.

# BEEF AND POTATO STACK

*This is a very adaptable dish. Sausage, sweet or hot, can be substituted for some of the beef. Barbecue sauce instead of spaghetti sauce gives a different flavor. A salad and some good bread completes this meal.*

2 large potatoes, peeled and thinly
    sliced
1½ lb. lean ground beef
½ cup seasoned breadcrumbs
1 medium onion, finely chopped
2 cloves garlic, finely chopped

1 egg, lightly beaten
salt and pepper to taste
1 tsp. dried mixed Italian herbs, optional
¾ cup thick spaghetti sauce, any flavor
1 cup shredded Monterey Jack cheese

Preheat oven to 375°. Parboil potatoes in salted water for 5 minutes. They should be undercooked. Drain and set aside.

In a medium bowl, combine beef, breadcrumbs, onion, garlic, egg, seasonings and ½ cup of the spaghetti sauce. Spoon ½ of the mixture into a nonstick loaf pan with a trivet (so fat can drain off). Spread ½ of the cheese over meat; spread sliced potatoes over cheese. Top with remaining meat. Bake for about 45 minutes. Top with remaining spaghetti sauce and remaining cheese. Bake for an additional 15 minutes. Let stand for 10 minutes.

# CHILI MEAT LOAF

*This loaf, served with corn or tortilla chips, is a meal in itself. Even kids eat it with gusto. If there is too much meat mixture to fit your pan, make a small loaf (or two) as well; it makes a wonderful lunch.*

1 tbs. vegetable oil
1 medium onion, chopped
2 cloves garlic, minced
1 red bell pepper, coarsely chopped
1 jalapeño pepper, cored, seeded and
    minced, or 1 jar (4 oz.) chopped
    jalapeños
salt and pepper to taste
2 tbs. chili powder (more or less)
2 tsp. ground cumin
1 tsp. fennel seed, optional
2 tbs. chopped fresh basil, or 2 tsp. dried
2 tbs. chopped fresh parsley (prefer flat-
    leaf Italian-style)

1 can (28 oz.) crushed or sliced Italian-
    style tomatoes, partially drained
1 can (8 oz.) tomato sauce
2 lb. lean ground beef
2 eggs, lightly beaten
1 cup plain or Italian-seasoned
    breadcrumbs
1 can (1 lb.) pinto beans, rinsed and
    drained
1 cup corn kernels, fresh, frozen or
    canned, drained, uncooked
1 cup mild or medium-hot salsa, warmed
1/2 cup shredded Monterey Jack cheese

Preheat oven to 350°. Lightly oil your largest loaf pan, a nonstick loaf pan with a trivet (so fat can drain off) or two smaller pans.

In a large skillet, heat oil and sauté onion, garlic, pepper and jalapeños until vegetables are soft. Remove from heat and transfer to a large bowl. Add seasonings, tomatoes, tomato sauce, beef, eggs, breadcrumbs, beans and corn. Mix well. Pack into loaf pan and bake for 1 hour or until done. Turn out onto a warm platter. Spread with salsa. Sprinkle cheese on top.

# MEXICALI BAKE

*This combination is more delicious than the sum of its parts. You can add (chopped celery, grated cheddar, grated zucchini) or subtract (seasonings).*

2 lb. lean ground beef
1 can (15 oz.) chopped Italian-style
   tomatoes
½ cup finely chopped green or red bell
   pepper
1 medium onion, finely chopped
1 cup crushed corn chips or tortilla chips
2 cloves garlic, finely chopped

1 tbs. chopped fresh jalapeño pepper,
   or 2 tbs. canned
1 tsp. ground cumin
salt and pepper to taste
1 tsp. dried oregano
¼ cup chopped fresh cilantro
2 eggs, lightly beaten

## TOPPING
1 can (15 oz.) tomato sauce
2 tbs. brown sugar
¼ tsp. cayenne pepper (or more)
½ tsp. ground cumin
salt and pepper to taste

Preheat oven to 350°. Spray a loaf pan with nonstick cooking spray or oil lightly if you plan to unmold the loaf. If you are spooning it out, you can omit this step.

Combine all ingredients for meat loaf. In a separate bowl, combine all topping ingredients. Add ½ cup topping to meat mixture. If it seems too wet, add more crushed corn chips. Mix well. Place meat mixture into loaf pan and bake for 45 minutes. Spread with remaining topping and bake for an additional 10 minutes until done. Let loaf stand for about 10 minutes before slicing.

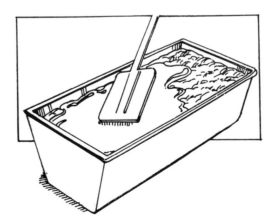

# SURPRISE MEAT LOAF

*This loaf looks innocent enough, but it can pack a wallop. Heat can be varied to suit individual taste.*

1½ lb. lean ground beef
1½ cups unsweetened cereal flakes
   (wheat or corn), slightly crushed
1 cup tomato juice (or V-8)
1 egg, lightly beaten

1 small onion, chopped
2 cloves garlic, chopped
salt and pepper to taste
1 tsp. ground cumin, optional

**TOPPINGS**
½ cup mild or hot salsa
chopped fresh cilantro

Preheat oven to 350°. Combine all meat loaf ingredients. Place mixture in a nonstick 9-x-5-inch loaf pan. Spread salsa on top. Bake for 1 hour or until done. Let loaf stand for 10 minutes. Lift out loaf with two spatulas and place on a serving platter; the salsa should remain on top. Top with chopped cilantro.

# APPLESAUCE MEAT LOAF

*A simple meat loaf has a great flavor. Homemade applesauce is a real plus.*

1½ lb. lean ground beef
½ lb. lean ground pork
1 medium onion, chopped
½ cup chopped red bell pepper
1 cup applesauce
1 egg, lightly beaten
1 cup breadcrumbs
3 tbs. ketchup, regular or hot
salt and pepper to taste
2 tbs. ketchup for topping, optional

Preheat oven to 350°. Lightly spray a nonstick loaf pan. In a large bowl, combine all ingredients and mix well. Place mixture in pan and top with additional ketchup, if desired. Bake for 1 hour or until done. Let stand for a few minutes and turn out of pan.

# SWEET CHILDREN'S LOAF

*This is really enjoyed by people of all ages. Even people who say they don't like meat loaf (there still must be a few) like this. It makes a great sandwich filling.*

1 lb. lean ground beef
1 lb. lean ground pork (or use all beef)
1 egg, lightly beaten
½ cup minced onion
2 cloves garlic, minced
3 tbs. brown sugar

salt and pepper to taste
½ tsp. dry mustard
½ tsp. dry sage (or more), optional
½ cup ketchup
3 slices bread (any kind), torn into
    pieces and soaked in milk

**TOPPING**
1 cup ketchup
½ cup brown sugar

1 tsp. dry mustard
1 tbs. wine vinegar

Preheat oven to 350°. In a large bowl, combine all meat loaf ingredients, adding milk-soaked bread last. Mix well. Pack into a 9-x-5-inch nonstick loaf pan with a trivet (so fat can drain off). Combine topping ingredients and set aside. Bake loaf for about 45 minutes. Spread topping over loaf and return to oven for an additional 30 minutes. Let loaf stand for 10 minutes before slicing.

# CINNAMON-RAISIN HAM LOAF

*This is like a ham-and-Swiss on raisin bread, a delicious combination.*

1½ lb. lean ground ham (steak), all fat removed
2 eggs, lightly beaten
2 stalks celery, finely chopped
1 onion, finely chopped
2 cloves garlic, finely minced
1 cup seasoned breadcrumbs

4 slices raisin bread, toasted and crumbled
1¼ cups ketchup
2 tbs. spicy brown mustard
salt and pepper to taste
½ cup grated Swiss cheese (prefer Gruyère)

**TOPPING**
3-4 slices Gruyère cheese

Preheat oven to 325°. Lightly oil a 9-x-5-inch loaf pan. In a large bowl, combine all meat loaf ingredients and press into pan. Bake for 45 minutes to 1 hour. Remove loaf and lay slices of cheese on top, slightly overlapping them. Return loaf to oven until cheese browns. Let stand for 10 minutes before slicing.

# ITALIAN SAUSAGE MEAT LOAF

*Italian sausage (mild or hot) makes this company fare. You can vary the proportions of meat to sausage, or substitute ground turkey for the beef. If you use a loaf pan with a trivet, most of the fat will drip through the holes.*

1 lb. very lean ground beef (prefer sirloin)
¾ lb. Italian sausage, casing removed
⅔ cup breadcrumbs (or more if firmer loaf is desired)
2 eggs, lightly beaten
2 cloves garlic, chopped
1 medium onion, chopped
⅓ cup ketchup
2-3 drops Tabasco Sauce
2 tbs. Worcestershire sauce
salt and pepper to taste
½ tbs. dried mixed Italian herbs
1 cup vegetable juice (V-8) or tomato juice

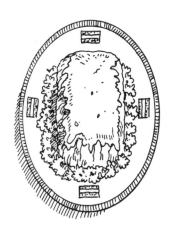

## TOPPING

1/3 cup ketchup
2 drops Tabasco Sauce
1 tbs. brown sugar
1 tsp. dried shredded onion flakes, or 1/2 cup chopped onion
1 clove garlic, chopped

Preheat oven to 350°. In a large bowl, combine beef and sausage thoroughly; it is easier to use your hand than a spoon. Add all other meat loaf ingredients. Place in a loaf pan. In a small bowl, combine topping ingredients. Spread over meat loaf. Bake for 1 hour or until done. Drain fat. If using pan with trivet, let loaf stand for 15 minutes. Unmold.

# GREEK-STYLE YOGURT MEAT LOAF

*Serve this with a good bread (Greek loaf, if possible) and a salad. Potatoes or rice and a Greek salad complement this dish.*

2 tbs. olive oil
1 cup chopped red or green bell pepper
1 clove garlic, chopped
3 tbs. minced shallots
1 small red onion, chopped
½ cup Madeira or sherry
3-4 slices good-quality bread, torn into large pieces
2 lb. very lean ground beef
salt and pepper to taste
2 tbs. chopped fresh oregano, or 1 tsp. dried
2 tsp. dried dill weed
2 eggs, lightly beaten
½ cup grated imported Parmesan cheese
1½ cups sour cream or plain yogurt (or 1 cup yogurt and ½ cup sour cream)
¼ cup prepared horseradish

## TOPPING
1 cup plain yogurt
1 tsp. dried dill weed
3 tbs. chopped red onion
¼ cup pitted black olives, optional

Preheat oven to 350°. Lightly oil a loaf pan. In a medium skillet, heat oil and sauté pepper, garlic, shallots and onion until soft. Set aside to cool. Place Madeira in a large bowl. Add bread and soak until all moisture is absorbed. Mash bread with a fork. Add beef, sautéed vegetables, seasonings, eggs and Parmesan cheese. In a small bowl, combine sour cream and horseradish. Add to meat mixture. Mix well and place in a loaf pan. Bake for 45 minutes to 1 hour, until done. Let stand for a few minutes before slicing. Combine topping ingredients and spoon on meat loaf.

# SPICY MEAT LOAF WITH MUSHROOMS AND TOMATOES

*Fresh tomato pieces baked into this loaf make it particularly juicy. Served cold, it makes a most satisfying sandwich.*

1 tbs. vegetable oil
1 medium onion, minced
½ cup minced celery
1 large clove garlic, minced
1 cup (or more) sliced mushrooms
　　(prefer portobello)
1 lb. lean ground beef
1 egg, lightly beaten
¾ cup breadcrumbs

salt and pepper to taste
2 tbs. Worcestershire sauce
1 tsp. paprika
1 tsp. dry mustard
1 tsp. ground cumin
3-4 plum tomatoes, coarsely chopped
　　(if substituting regular tomatoes,
　　remove some seeds and juice)
chopped fresh cilantro for garnish

Preheat oven to 350°. Heat oil in a skillet. Sauté onion, celery, garlic and mushrooms until soft. Transfer to a bowl, Combine onion mixture with all other ingredients, except tomato pieces. Mix well; add tomato pieces last. Pack into a nonstick loaf pan, pushing pieces of tomato down into mixture. Bake for about 45 to 55 minutes. Top with cilantro.

# GRITS AND SAUSAGE BAKE

*This satisfying loaf can be prepared the night before and heated at the last minute. Good for breakfast or brunch; add a salad and you have an easy lunch or supper.*

2 cups water
½ cup quick-cooking grits
2 cups shredded sharp (or extra-sharp) cheddar cheese
1 lb. mild or hot pork sausage
2 cloves garlic, finely minced
4 eggs, lightly beaten

1 cup milk
½ tsp. dried thyme
2 tbs. chopped fresh dill weed, or 2 tsp. dried
1 tbs. chopped fresh chives, or 1 tsp. dried
salt and pepper to taste

Preheat oven to 350° (if cooking immediately). Lightly grease a nonstick or glass loaf pan. Bring water to a boil; stir in grits. Return to boil; reduce heat and cook for about 4 minutes, stirring occasionally. Mixture should be thick. Remove from heat; add cheese and stir until melted.

In a skillet, sauté sausage and garlic until sausage is cooked through. Drain on paper towels, and crumble. Combine eggs, milk and seasonings. Add grits, a little at a time (to prevent lumps), cooked sausage and garlic to egg mixture. Pour into prepared loaf pan. Cover and refrigerate up to 24 hours. Bake, uncovered, for 50 minutes or until set. The loaf should puff up and turn golden brown.

# DINER MEAT LOAF

*This meat loaf is an old friend. It tastes like something you would be served in a diner, but with a more interesting combination of flavors. This recipe makes 2 loaves that can be frozen baked or unbaked.*

## SAUCE

½ cup ketchup
2 tbs. water
1 tbs. sugar
1 tbs. soy sauce

1 tsp. paprika
salt and pepper to taste
½ tsp. garlic powder
½ tsp. onion powder

Combine sauce ingredients and set aside.

2½ lb. lean ground beef (more or less)
1 pkg. dry onion soup mix
1 tsp. dried oregano
2 tbs. chopped fresh parsley
½ cup pickle relish
1 tbs. Worcestershire sauce
⅓ cup ketchup

salt and pepper to taste
3 eggs, lightly beaten
1 can (13 oz.) evaporated milk (can be nonfat)
¾ cup cornmeal
3½ cups dry seasoned breadcrumbs
¼ cup water

Preheat oven to 350°. Lightly oil two 9-x-5-inch loaf pans.

Combine all meat loaf ingredients, except water, and place in prepared loaf pan. Bake for about 30 minutes. Top with ½ cup of the sauce and bake for another 15 minutes; brush with remaining sauce. As soon as meat loaf is removed from oven, pour about ¼ cup water on top of loaf. Let stand for 10 minutes. Remove loaf to a platter.

# BEEF-SAUSAGE MEAT LOAF

*This recipe makes two 8-x-4-inch loaves. Served cold, it makes particularly good sandwiches. The garlic, onion, pepper and celery can be minced in a food processor.*

2 tbs. butter
3 large cloves garlic, finely minced
1 large onion, finely chopped
1 small red or green bell pepper (or both), finely chopped
1 large stalk celery, finely chopped
1½ lb. lean ground beef
½ lb. hot Italian sausage meat

¾ cup breadcrumbs (prefer seasoned Italian-style)
2 eggs, lightly beaten
½ cup ketchup (more for top, optional)
2 tbs. milk
2 tsp. Worcestershire sauce
salt and pepper to taste
¼ tsp. cayenne pepper

Preheat oven to 375°. Place rack in center of oven. In a small skillet, melt butter and sauté vegetables until soft, about 5 minutes. Transfer to a large bowl. Combine with all other ingredients; do not overmix. Pack into two 8-x-4-inch loaf pans, preferably with trivets so fat can drain away. Top with additional ketchup, if using. Bake for about 1 hour or until done. Serve hot or at room temperature.

# GERMAN MEAT LOAF

*This loaf is simple and satisfying. Use a nonstick loaf pan with a trivet and drain away fat.*

2 cups coarse breadcrumbs (prefer rye bread)
¾ cup milk
1 large onion, finely chopped
2 cloves garlic, finely chopped
1 lb. lean ground beef
½ lb. lean ground pork
¾ cup grated imported Parmesan cheese
2 eggs, lightly beaten
1 tsp. fennel seed
1 tsp. dried mixed Italian herbs, optional
salt and pepper to taste
chopped fresh parsley for garnish

Preheat oven to 375°. Combine breadcrumbs and milk. Let stand for 10 minutes until milk has been absorbed. Toss breadcrumbs with remaining ingredients. Do not overmix. Place mixture in a loaf pan and bake for about 45 minutes until done. Cool for 10 minutes. Unmold. Garnish.

# ORIENTAL MEAT LOAF

*I'm not sure you could find this in any part of the Orient, but the combination suggests the Far-Eastern flavor. Serve it with rice. You may want to go easy on the hoisin sauce; it is an acquired taste.*

1 tbs. peanut oil
½ cup finely chopped onion
2 cloves garlic, finely minced
1 red or green bell pepper, chopped
1 tsp. minced ginger root (or more)
2 lb. lean ground beef
1½ cups fresh breadcrumbs
¼ cup soy sauce
2 tbs. rice vinegar
2 tbs. sugar

**TOPPING**
1 cup jellied cranberry sauce
½ cup hoisin sauce (or less)
¼ cup honey
1 tbs. rice vinegar
2 tbs. chopped peanuts, optional

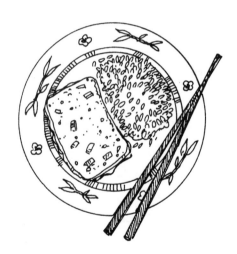

Preheat oven to 350°. In a small skillet, heat oil. Sauté onion, garlic, red pepper and ginger for a few minutes, until vegetables are tender. In a large bowl, combine all ingredients for meat loaf. Place meat mixture in a nonstick loaf pan with a trivet and bake for 1 hour, until done.

In a small saucepan over low heat, mix topping ingredients until cranberry sauce is dissolved. Place sauce on top of meat loaf and cook for another 10 minutes. Let meat loaf stand for 10 minutes before slicing.

# PIZZA IN A LOAF

*This can be varied to suit individual pizza tastes. Add sausage or red and green peppers, anchovies, mushrooms or pepperoni. Served in a pita bread with melted mozzarella, it makes an irresistible sandwich. Or serve on toasted English muffins.*

½ lb. sausage, optional
1 lb. lean ground beef
2 cups pizza sauce or seasoned tomato sauce
¾ cup Italian-seasoned breadcrumbs
½ cup sliced ripe olives
½ cup finely chopped onion

1 clove garlic, minced
salt and pepper to taste
1 tsp. dried mixed Italian herbs
pita bread
shredded mozzarella cheese
grated Parmesan cheese

Preheat oven to 350°. If using sausage, remove skin, place in a skillet and sauté for a few minutes to get rid of some of the fat. Drain sausage well and combine with remaining ingredients, except pita bread and cheeses. Mix until thoroughly combined. Place in a nonstick loaf pan with a trivet to drain most of the fat. Bake for 50 minutes or until done. Let stand in pan for 5 minutes. Spoon into pita bread, while still hot, with some shredded mozzarella and Parmesan cheeses.

# BEEFY HAM AND CHEESE BAKE

*This simple loaf is a family favorite. Kids of all ages love it. It can be eaten warm or cold and makes a very tasty sandwich filling.*

2 lb. lean ground beef (can use part Italian sausage)
2 cloves garlic, finely minced
¾ cup Italian-seasoned breadcrumbs
2 cups seasoned tomato sauce
salt and pepper to taste
1 tsp. dried mixed Italian herbs
¼ lb. boiled ham, thinly sliced
¼ lb. mozzarella cheese, shredded
½ cup grated imported Parmesan cheese

Preheat oven to 350°. Use a loaf pan with a trivet to drain away most of the fat. Mix together meat, garlic, breadcrumbs, tomato sauce and seasonings. Place ½ of the mixture in loaf pan. Add sliced ham. Sprinkle with mozzarella cheese and ¼ cup of the Parmesan. Place remaining beef mixture on top. Bake for 40 minutes until done. Add remaining ¼ cup Parmesan during last 5 minutes of baking.

# BRUNCH HAM AND BROCCOLI BAKE

*Make 2 loaves and serve 8 people for brunch, or save 1 loaf for later. This recipe can be prepared the day before. Add other vegetables (mushrooms, peppers); it just seems to improve. Sharp cheddar can replace all or part of the Swiss cheese.*

1 medium onion, chopped
3 cups chopped fresh broccoli (can use
    frozen in a pinch)
1 tbs. butter
1 loaf bread, day-old, about 1 lb. (Italian,
    French, whole grain), slices ½-inch thick
2 cups diced cooked ham
4 eggs, lightly beaten
2 cups milk (can use part half-and-half)
1 tsp. dry mustard
salt and white pepper to taste
8 oz. (2 cups) coarsely grated Swiss cheese
paprika

Preheat oven to 350° if you are baking the loaves right away. Generously grease 2 glass 9-x-5-inch loaf pans.

Stir-fry onion and broccoli in a little butter for about 5 minutes. Broccoli should be underdone. If using frozen broccoli, just defrost; no need to cook. Place bread slices in bottom of loaf pan. Sprinkle with some of the broccoli-onion mixture and some of the ham. Repeat. Top with bread slices; use the most attractive slices for the top. Combine eggs, milk, seasonings and 1 cup of the Swiss cheese. Pour over top. Cover and place in refrigerator for up to 24 hours.

Bake uncovered for 45 minutes. Add remaining 1 cup cheese, sprinkle with paprika and bake for another 15 minutes. Serve immediately.

# HAM-APPLE MEAT LOAF WITH THYME

*Do not add salt to this before tasting. The ham may be saltier than you think.*

¾ lb. lean ground beef
¾ lb. ground cooked ham (use food
    processor)
1 cup applesauce (prefer homemade)
½ cup white wine or water
¼ cup dry sherry
2 cups cubed day-old bread, small
    cubes (prefer French or Italian)

¾ cup chopped onion
1 egg, lightly beaten
1 tsp. dried thyme, or 1 tbs. fresh
½ tsp. cinnamon
pepper to taste

**TOPPING**
1 cup applesauce flavored with 1 tbs. fresh or ½ tsp. dried thyme

Preheat oven to 350°. Spray pan with nonstick cooking spray if you plan to unmold the loaf. If you are spooning it out, you may omit this step. In a large bowl, combine all meat loaf ingredients. Mix well. Let it stand for about 10 minutes to give bread time to absorb other ingredients. Place mixture in prepared loaf pan. Bake for about 50 minutes, until done. Serve with thyme-flavored applesauce.

# MIDDLE EASTERN LAMB LOAF WITH COUSCOUS

*Uncooked bulgur wheat can be substituted for couscous. Follow the same instructions. This loaf makes a hearty main dish. All you need is a salad and some Middle Eastern bread for a complete meal. If you are concerned about cholesterol, use a nonstick loaf pan with a trivet; most of the fat will drip through the holes.*

¾ cup uncooked couscous
3 cups boiling salted water
1½ lb. lean ground lamb
1 medium onion, chopped
2 cloves garlic, chopped
½ cup pine nuts
½ cup raisins
½ cup apple juice or apple brandy

1½ tsp. cinnamon
1½ tsp. ground cumin
1 tsp. dried mint
2 tbs. chopped fresh cilantro
salt and pepper to taste
chopped fresh cilantro for garnish,
    optional
yogurt, optional

Preheat oven to 350°. Place couscous in large bowl. Cover with water and let stand for about 10 minutes until water is absorbed. Drain (if necessary) and set aside. Combine lamb with remaining ingredients; add couscous last. Mix well. Transfer mixture into a 9-x-5-inch loaf pan. Cover with foil; bake for about 30 minutes. Uncover and bake for another 15 minutes or until done. Let stand for about 10 minutes. Unmold. Garnish. Serve with yogurt, if desired.

# TAILGATE MEAT LOAF

*This is perfect picnic fare. Most of these ingredients can be found in your pantry, so making it can be a last-minute decision. If baked in a nonstick loaf pan with a trivet, most of the fat will drain away.*

2 lb. lean ground beef (can use part sweet or Italian sausage)
1 cup Italian-seasoned breadcrumbs
1 medium onion, finely chopped
2 cloves garlic, finely chopped
½ cup beef stock (or water, in an emergency)
½ cup dry red wine
1 can (8 oz.) tomato sauce
1 tbs. Worcestershire sauce
1 tbs. steak sauce
salt and pepper to taste

Preheat oven to 350°. Combine all ingredients and mix well. Pack into a loaf pan and bake for 1 hour. Remove from pan and drain juices. Serve hot or cold.

# TEX-MEX CORN AND BEAN MEAT BAKE

*Add a loaf of cornbread and a green salad and you have a complete meal. If it is too much meat mixture for the loaf pan, make a small extra loaf. A fabulous lunch!*

2 tbs. vegetable oil
½ lb. lean ground beef (or more)
1 medium onion, chopped
2 cloves garlic, minced
½ cup chopped red or green bell
    pepper (or more)
kernels from 2 large ears corn (about
    1½ cups), uncooked
1 can (1 lb.) red kidney beans, rinsed
    and drained

1 can (1 lb.) stewed tomatoes
1 jar (4 oz.) jalapeño peppers, optional
1 tbs. chili powder (or more)
salt and pepper to taste
2-3 drops Tabasco Sauce
1 cup water
½ cup cornmeal
1 cup pitted black olives, sliced
1 cup shredded sharp cheddar cheese

Preheat oven to 375° (if baking right away). In a large skillet, heat oil and sauté beef, onion, garlic and peppers for 5 minutes. Add corn, kidney beans, tomatoes, jalapeños and seasonings. Simmer for 5 minutes. Stir water into cornmeal slowly, to prevent lumps, and add to skillet. Cover and simmer for a few minutes. Add olives. Transfer ingredients to a 9-x-5-inch loaf pan. You can refrigerate for several hours or overnight, or bake immediately. Bake for about 45 minutes. Top with shredded cheese and bake for another 5 minutes. Serve hot.

# MUSHROOM GOAT CHEESE MEAT LOAF

*This luscious meat loaf is an easy company dish. A fresh tomato salad and a French bread are perfect complements. Use a clay pan if possible.*

1 lb. lean ground beef
1 lb. ground veal
1 clove garlic, finely chopped
2 eggs, lightly beaten
¾ cup breadcrumbs (or enough to give loaf a firm consistency)
½ cup grated imported Romano cheese
½ cup ketchup

1 tbs. Dijon mustard (or more)
1 tsp. dried mixed Italian herbs
½ cup chopped fresh parsley (prefer flat-leaf Italian-style)
⅛ tsp. hot sauce
salt and pepper to taste
4 oz. good-quality goat cheese (prefer French), room temperature

## FILLING

2 tbs. butter
1 tbs. olive oil
2 cloves garlic, finely chopped
2 large shallots, finely chopped
½ lb. portobello (or other "wild") mushrooms, sliced

2 tbs. chopped fresh basil, or 1 tsp. dried
1 tbs. chopped fresh thyme, or ½ tsp. dried
salt and pepper to taste

Preheat oven to 350°. Lightly oil a 9-x-5-inch loaf pan. Combine beef and veal and all the other meat loaf ingredients, except goat cheese. Mix well. Set aside.

For the filling: In a medium skillet, heat 1 tbs. butter and olive oil. Sauté garlic, shallots and mushrooms for a few minutes, until vegetables are limp. Add seasonings and remaining 1 tbs. butter and cook, stirring often, until vegetables are slightly brown, about 3 to 4 minutes. Set aside.

Place ½ of the meat mixture in loaf pan. Spread goat cheese over meat. Spread vegetable filling over goat cheese and top with remaining meat mixture. Bake for 1 hour or until done. Let loaf stand for about 10 minutes before slicing and serving.

# LOAVES WITH VEGETABLES, PASTA AND GRAINS

# ZUCCHINI CARROT LOAF

*This recipe evolved from my mother's squash pancakes. In my streamlined version there is less oil, fewer eggs and more seasoning. You can use yellow summer squash in place of some of the zucchini. It is a great lunch.*

4 cups coarsely shredded zucchini,
  peeled if tough skin (3 or 4 zucchini)
2 cups coarsely shredded carrots
½ cup chopped green onions, including
  some green
2 cloves garlic, finely minced
½ cup flour (or more)
2 tsp. baking powder
salt and pepper to taste

¾ cup grated imported Parmesan cheese
3 tbs. vegetable oil
2 eggs, lightly beaten
1 tsp. dried dill
2 tbs. dried chives
1 tsp. dried basil
½ tsp. dried oregano
2 tbs. chopped fresh parsley (prefer flat-
  leaf Italian-syle)

Preheat oven to 350°. Oil a 9-x-5-inch loaf pan. Use a food processor, if possible, to grate zucchini and carrots. Using your hands, squeeze out excess moisture from grated zucchini and carrots (important). Discard liquid. Combine vegetables with remaining ingredients. Mix thoroughly with your hands or with a large spoon. The mixture should be somewhat loose. Spoon into prepared loaf pan. Bake for about 50 minutes or until firm. Serve hot or cold, with drinks or as a vegetable side dish.

# BAKED VEGETABLE MELANGE

*These ordinary vegetables become something special when combined in this way. The proportions don't seem to matter. You can add mushrooms or broccoli. Cheddar cheese can be substituted for the Parmesan, or use both.*

2 tbs. vegetable oil
2 cups zucchini or any summer squash
    (or combination), sliced about
    1/4-inch thick
1 cup diced red or green bell pepper
1 1/2 cups thinly sliced carrots
2 stalks celery, sliced
1/2 cup chopped green onions, including
    some green
2 cloves garlic, minced

1 tsp. dried mixed Italian herbs (or less)
salt and pepper to taste
1 cup sour cream (or all or part plain
    yogurt)
1/2 cup grated imported Parmesan cheese
3 tbs. chopped fresh dill weed or
    parsley (prefer flat leaf Italian-style)
1/4 cup imported Parmesan cheese
1/4 cup Italian-seasoned breadcrumbs

Preheat oven to 350°. Lightly oil a nonstick 9-x-5-inch loaf pan. In a large skillet, heat oil. Sauté vegetables for a few minutes, until zucchini wilts and onions soften. Stir in remaining ingredients, except 1/4 cup Parmesan and 1/4 cup breadcrumbs. Mix well and transfer to prepared loaf pan. Sprinkle with cheese and breadcrumbs. Bake for 20 to 30 minutes. Do not overbake; vegetables should still be firm.

# LOW FAT VEGETABLE LOAF

*This satisfying vegetable dish can include other vegetables (sliced mushrooms, cubed potatoes) that "need eating."*

1½ cups coarsely chopped carrots
1 cup coarsely chopped celery
2 cups coarsely chopped broccoli
    (include some stems)
1 cup green bean pieces, ¼-inch
1 tbs. vegetable oil
1 small onion, chopped

2 cloves garlic, chopped
1 cup breadcrumbs
1 egg, lightly beaten
salt and pepper to taste
1 tsp. dried basil, or 2 tbs. fresh
½ tsp. nutmeg or ground ginger

Preheat oven to 350°. Grease a loaf pan. Combine chopped vegetables. Heat oil and sauté onion and garlic for about 2 minutes. Add chopped vegetables and stir to coat. Remove from heat. Add breadcrumbs, egg and seasonings. Place in loaf pan and bake for about 45 minutes, until firm. Let stand for 10 minutes. Unmold. Serve hot or at room temperature.

# BROCCOLI WITH CHEESE

*This simple preparation takes broccoli out of the ordinary class. It goes with many meats and makes a great lunch. If you use a glass loaf pan, it can be reheated in the microwave.*

1-2 lb. fresh broccoli
½ cup cottage cheese (or a little more)
1 egg, lightly beaten
1 small onion, minced
¼ cup shredded Swiss cheese (prefer
   Jarlsberg)

salt and white pepper to taste
2 drops Tabasco Sauce
¼ cup breadcrumbs
2 tbs. butter, melted
paprika

Preheat oven to 325°. Lightly butter a glass loaf pan. Peel broccoli stems. Cut stems into 1-inch pieces. Leave florets whole or in large pieces. Steam over boiling salted water for no more than 5 minutes. Broccoli should be undercooked. Drain. Combine remaining ingredients except breadcrumbs, butter and paprika. Mix well. Place broccoli in prepared loaf pan. Spoon sauce evenly over broccoli. Mix breadcrumbs and butter and sprinkle over cheese mixture. Cover dish tightly with aluminum foil. Bake until cheese topping is set, about 20 minutes. Remove foil and sprinkle with paprika.

# SWEET POTATO VEGETABLE LOAF WITH CHEESE

*This adaptable loaf can be changed with the season and what is in the refrigerator. Carrots can replace the zucchini; fresh spinach can replace the broccoli. Be sure to use the sweet potato; it gives the loaf its character.*

1 tbs. vegetable oil
1 cup finely chopped onion
1 large clove garlic, minced
2 sweet potatoes (about 1/2 lb.), peeled
   and shredded
2 cups chopped fresh broccoli, or 2
   pkg. (10 oz. each) frozen chopped
   broccoli, defrosted
1 cup shredded zucchini

1 cup seasoned breadcrumbs
2 eggs, lightly beaten
1/2 cup grated imported Parmesan cheese
1 cup shredded Monterey Jack or Swiss
   cheese
1 tsp. dried dill weed
1 tsp. chopped fresh chives, optional
salt and pepper to taste

Preheat oven to 350°. Grease a nonstick loaf pan. Heat oil in a large skillet. Add onion and garlic and all vegetables; cook until softened, stirring occasionally. In a large bowl, combine vegetable mixture with breadcrumbs, eggs, cheeses and seasonings. Mix thoroughly and spoon into a loaf pan. Bake for about 50 minutes, until loaf is brown and firm. Let stand for about 10 minutes. Unmold.

# POTATO CARROT KUGEL

*This kugel is an interesting side dish for meat or chicken. You can add a small zucchini to the mixture for additional color. Or substitute zucchini for all of the carrots.*

3 cups grated raw potatoes (4 or 5
    medium)
1 large onion, grated
1 cup grated carrots
1 small zucchini, grated, optional
2 eggs, lightly beaten

2 tbs. vegetable oil
1/2 cup flour
1/2 tsp. baking powder
salt and pepper to taste
1 tsp. chopped fresh chives, optional
1 tbs. chopped fresh dill weed

Preheat oven to 350°. Grease a 9-x-5-inch loaf pan. Combine potatoes, onion, carrots and zucchini, if using. Squeeze out moisture with hands over a bowl, saving liquid. Combine all ingredients including potato starch that will collect in bottom of bowl (pour off and discard remaining liquid). Mix well. Spoon into prepared loaf pan and bake until brown on top, about 1 hour. Serve hot.

# POTATOES AND CHEESE

*This loaf is a perfect accompaniment to baked ham or turkey. It can be made ahead of time and reheated or served at room temperature.*

6 medium red potatoes, boiled until almost tender, peeled and chilled
2 cups shredded sharp cheddar cheese
1½ cups sour cream or plain yogurt (or half of each)
1 medium onion, chopped
salt and pepper to taste
2 tbs. butter, cut into pieces

Preheat oven to 350°. Generously butter a 9-x-5-inch loaf pan. Coarsely grate boiled potatoes. Place in a large bowl with remaining ingredients, except butter. Mix thoroughly, and transfer mixture to prepared loaf pan. Dot with butter and bake until golden brown on top, about 30 minutes.

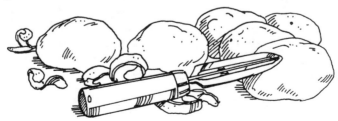

# SCALLOPED POTATOES AND KALE

*This dish goes very well with chicken or meat. Even people who avoid green vegetables love it. Eaten cold, it's a great snack for the next day. Use a food processor to slice the potatoes if you can. Use real butter instead of margarine; here, the butter taste is important.*

½ lb. kale, heavy stems removed
½ cup water
4 cups new potatoes, peeled and thinly
   sliced
2 cloves garlic, minced

½ cup thinly sliced green onions,
   including some green
1 cup grated Swiss cheese
½ cup butter, cut into small pieces
½ cup dry white wine, optional
½ cup chicken stock (use 1 cup stock
   if you do not use wine)
2 tbs. chopped fresh dill weed, or 1 tsp.
   dried
salt and pepper to taste
2 tsp. minced chives
2 eggs, lightly beaten
½ cup half-and-half

Preheat oven to 400°. Generously butter a 9-x-5-inch nonstick loaf pan.

Rinse kale and shake off excess water. Place in a medium saucepan with 1/2 cup water. Cover and cook over medium heat for 5 minutes. Drain and cool. Using your hands, squeeze out remaining water. Chop kale coarsely and set aside. Parboil potatoes in salted water for about 3 minutes. Drain well.

Place 1/3 of the sliced potatoes in prepared loaf pan. Layer 1/2 of the kale leaves, 1/2 of the garlic and green onions, 1/3 of the Swiss cheese and butter pieces, another 1/3 of the potatoes, remaining 1/2 of the kale, garlic and green onions, and another 1/3 of the cheese and butter; top with last 1/3 of the potatoes. Combine remaining ingredients, including last 1/3 of the cheese and butter; pour over potato mixture. Tap loaf pan on a flat surface to make liquid mixture go to bottom. Bake for 45 minutes, until top is set and crusty, and liquid has been absorbed. If it browns too quickly, cover with aluminum foil during the last 10 minutes of baking. Let stand for 10 minutes. Drain off any remaining liquid.

# LENTIL MUSHROOM LOAF WITH POTATO FILLING

*This is a complete meal or a great addition to a buffet. It can also be used as a side dish. The potato filling adds an interesting contrast in textures.*

1 cup uncooked lentils
4 cups salted water
1 tbs. vegetable oil
2 cloves garlic, minced
½ lb. mushrooms, sliced

1 pkg. (10 oz.) frozen chopped spinach, thawed and squeezed dry (important)
1 tbs. soy sauce
dash nutmeg
salt and pepper to taste
1 cup grated Gruyère cheese

## POTATO FILLING

1 tbs. vegetable oil
1 cup chopped onion
¼ cup breadcrumbs
1 cup coarsely mashed potato (about 1 large potato)

seasoned salt and pepper to taste
½ tsp. dried thyme
½ tsp. dried basil
chopped fresh cilantro or parsley for garnish

Rinse lentils thoroughly and sort to remove any small stones. Place in a heavy saucepan with 4 cups salted water. Bring to a boil, lower heat and simmer, covered, until lentils are tender, about 45 minutes. Drain.

Preheat oven to 350°. Lightly oil a 9-x-5-inch glass loaf pan.

In a large skillet, heat oil. Add garlic and mushrooms. Sauté until mushrooms are wilted. Stir in all ingredients, except cheese. Cook until mixture is heated through and well combined. Stir in cheese and mix lightly.

Prepare potato filling: In a skillet, heat oil, add onion and sauté until golden brown. Add remaining filling ingredients and sauté over low heat for about 5 minutes, stirring occasionally.

Press about ⅔ of the lentil mixture into prepared loaf pan along sides and bottom, to form a shell. Place potato filling in lentil shell and top with reserved lentil mixture. Bake for about 45 minutes until top is crusty. Remove loaf to a rack and let cool for about 10 minutes. Unmold onto a platter and garnish with chopped cilantro.

# THREE BEAN BAKE

*Beans and cheese, served with couscous or bulgur wheat, make a satisfying main dish. The combination can also be a savory accompaniment to grilled or roasted meat. This dish is simple to prepare, since the beans are already cooked.*

1 tbs. vegetable oil
1 medium onion, chopped
1 small green bell pepper, chopped
1 small red bell pepper, chopped
1 clove garlic, minced
1 can (15 oz.) kidney beans, rinsed
   and drained
1 can (15 oz.) great Northern beans
   or navy beans, rinsed and drained
1 can (15 oz.) garbanzo beans, rinsed
   and drained
1 can (15 oz.) Italian plum tomatoes,
   undrained
3 tbs. honey
½ cup soy sauce
1 tsp. chili powder (or more)

1 tsp. dried cilantro
1 tsp. paprika
1 tsp. dry mustard
½ cup grated sharp cheddar cheese
½ cup grated Monterey Jack cheese
chopped fresh cilantro for garnish
hot cooked couscous or bulgur wheat

Preheat oven to 400°. Lightly oil a 9-x-5-inch loaf pan. In a small skillet, heat oil. Add onion, peppers and garlic. Sauté until vegetables are limp. Remove from heat.

In a bowl, combine beans with vegetables and all other ingredients, except cheeses. Mix thoroughly. Pour bean mixture into prepared loaf pan; top with grated cheeses. Bake for 30 minutes or until cheeses are bubbly. Top with fresh cilantro. Serve with couscous or bulgur wheat, or as a side dish.

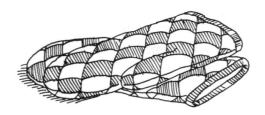

# SWEET POTATO STUFFING

*This versatile stuffing can be used with chicken (or turkey) or as a potato dish. It looks lovely on the table, and is a fine addition to a holiday meal. Or if you have some leftover sweet potatoes, you can whip this up in no time. Dried sage leaves have better flavor; use sage powder only in an emergency.*

2 tbs. unsalted butter
1/2 cup minced shallots or onions
3 cups coarsely mashed cooked or
  baked sweet potatoes (about 2 lb.)
3 cups dry bread cubes (plain or seasoned)
10-12 fresh sage leaves, or 1/2 tsp. dried
  sage, crumbled (or more)

2 tbs. minced fresh parsley (prefer
  flat-leaf Italian-style)
1/2 tsp. nutmeg (prefer freshly grated)
salt and pepper to taste
grated peel of 1 orange or lemon
1 cup chicken stock (more or less)

Preheat oven to 350°. Generously grease 1 large or 2 small loaf pans. Melt butter in a a skillet. Sauté shallots or onions until soft and translucent but not brown. Place sautéed shallots, potatoes, bread cubes, seasonings and orange peel in a large bowl. Add enough chicken broth to moisten; the mixture should be moist, but not soggy. Pack loosely into loaf pans and bake for about 30 minutes until heated through and slightly brown on top.

# HERB-VEGETABLE POLENTA STUFFING

*This stuffing can be made in a loaf pan and served with chicken, Cornish hens or turkey. Used as a side dish, it enhances any poultry entrée.*

4 cups chicken stock (prefer homemade)
1 cup yellow cornmeal
1 tsp. dried rosemary
½ tsp. dried thyme
½ tsp. dried sage leaves (not powder)
salt and pepper to taste
1 tbs. sugar

2 tbs. butter
2 tbs. olive oil
1 cup finely chopped celery
1 medium onion, finely chopped
1 cup (or more) coarsely chopped "wild" mushrooms (portobello or shiitake)

Preheat oven to 350°. Generously grease a heavy metal or clay loaf pan. In a large saucepan, bring chicken stock to a boil. Add cornmeal slowly (to prevent lumps) and whisk vigorously for a few minutes. Add seasonings and sugar. Cook over low heat for about 20 minutes, stirring occasionally.

Meanwhile, in a medium skillet, heat butter with olive oil and sauté celery, onion and mushrooms, until vegetables are translucent. Fold vegetables into cooked polenta. Place in prepared pan. Bake for about 30 minutes or until a crust forms on top.

# CORN PUDDING

*The ingredients are so simple, there is no reason why this pudding should taste so good. On a buffet, it always goes first. Leftovers (if there are any) keep very well. These loaves do not unmold easily, so bake in an attractive pan.*

¾ cup flour
3 tbs. sugar
1½ tsp. baking powder
3 eggs, room temperature, lightly
    beaten
2 cups milk (can use part half-and-half)
½ cup butter, melted and slightly cooled
kernels from 8 ears of corn, uncooked,
    or 3 cups corn kernels, frozen and
    slightly thawed

salt and pepper to taste
3 tbs. chopped fresh parsley
2 tbs. chopped fresh chives, or 2 tsp.
    dried
2 tbs. chopped fresh dill weed, or 2 tsp.
    dried
½ cup chopped green onions
1½ cups grated sharp cheddar cheese

Preheat oven to 350°. Grease loaf pans. In a large bowl, combine flour, sugar and baking powder. In another bowl, mix eggs, milk and melted butter. Blend into flour mixture. Add corn, salt and pepper, herbs, green onions and 1 cup of the cheese. Mix well. Pour into 2 loaf pans and bake until done, about 35 minutes. Sprinkle with remaining ½ cup cheese during the last 5 minutes of baking.

# NOODLE KUGEL

*This is the ultimate comfort food. Serve it as an accompaniment to poultry or meat dishes. With homemade apple sauce, it works as a nutritious dessert. A nonstick pan is preferred because this kugel may not want to unmold.*

½ lb. broad noodles
1 tbs. vegetable oil
3 eggs
½ cup brown sugar
½ tsp. cinnamon
¼ tsp. nutmeg

½ cup light raisins
½ cup chopped apple
¼ cup sliced almonds, lightly toasted
2 tbs. lemon juice
½ cup butter, melted

Preheat oven to 375°. Generously grease a 9-x-5-inch nonstick loaf pan. Cook noodles in boiling salted water for about 5 minutes (no more). Noodles should be undercooked. Drain, sprinkle with oil to prevent sticking, and set aside. Beat eggs with brown sugar until fluffy. Add noodles and all other ingredients and mix well. Transfer to loaf pan. Bake for about 50 minutes, until eggs are set and the loaf turns brown. Cool in pan.

# ROTINI WITH TWO CHEESES

*This is a take-off on macaroni and cheese, but much better. You can add almost any cooked vegetable to the mixture. Even vegetable haters can find no fault with carrots or zucchini served this way.*

½ lb. dried rotini pasta (or other short pasta)
1 tbs. salt, or to taste
¼ cup butter
¼ cup flour
seasoned salt and white pepper to taste
2 tsp. dry mustard
3 cups milk
1 tbs. Worcestershire sauce
2 tbs. butter
½ lb. mushrooms, sliced (prefer cremini)
4 green onions, chopped
½ cup shredded Swiss cheese (prefer Jarlsberg)
½ cup shredded sharp cheddar cheese
1 jar (4 oz.) chopped pimiento, undrained, optional
cooked vegetables — carrots, peas, zucchini, etc., optional
chopped parsley and chopped green onions for garnish

Preheat oven to 350°. Butter a 9-x-5-inch nonstick loaf pan. Add rotini and salt to a large pot of boiling water. Cook, stirring occasionally, for about 5 minutes. Rotini should be undercooked. Drain well and set aside.

While pasta is cooking, make sauce. Melt butter in a medium saucepan. Add flour, seasoned salt, pepper and mustard, and stir until smooth. Gradually add milk and whisk until mixture thickens and is bubbly. Cook for about 1 minute. Add Worcestershire sauce.

In a small skillet, melt butter and sauté mushrooms and green onions for a few minutes, until limp. Add to sauce. (If you are pushed for time, you can omit sautéing the mushrooms and onions. Just add them to the sauce as is.)

Remove from heat. Add cheeses and mix well. Combine cooked pasta and cheese sauce. Add pimiento and cooked vegetables, if using. Turn into prepared loaf pan and bake for about 45 minutes. Remove from oven and garnish.

# PESTO POLENTA WITH PINE NUTS

*Aged Asiago cheese is used like aged Parmesan. In a pinch, Parmesan can be substituted. The pine nuts add a special touch. The nuts can be toasted in a microwave, with or without a little olive oil.*

4 cups milk (can be 2%)
2 tbs. olive oil
1 tsp. honey (or a little more)
salt and pepper to taste

1 1/3 cups polenta or yellow cornmeal
1/4 cup pesto (prefer homemade)
3/4 cup grated aged Asiago cheese
1/2 cup pine nuts, lightly toasted

Preheat oven to 350°. Lightly oil a 9-x-5-inch loaf pan. In a heavy saucepan with a large surface area, heat milk, oil, honey, salt and pepper. Stir with a wire whisk until simmering. Add polenta slowly (to prevent lumps), stirring constantly with a wooden spoon until well combined. Cook, uncovered, over low heat for about 10 minutes, until polenta begins to pull away from sides of pan. Let polenta cool slightly.

Pour 1/2 of the polenta into prepared loaf pan and spread evenly. Spread pesto over polenta. Top with 1/2 of the cheese and 1/2 of the pine nuts. Top with remaining polenta, and sprinkle with remaining cheese and pine nuts. Bake for about 15 minutes until heated through. Let loaf stand for 5 minutes before serving.

# SPAGHETTI CASSEROLE AD HOC

*You can add or subtract from this recipe. Any cooked vegetable that needs eating can be added; broccoli or zucchini are particularly good. Seasonings can be changed; amount of meat can be reduced. This recipe freezes very well.*

1½ lb. ground beef or use part Italian
    sausage
1 medium onion, chopped
2 cloves garlic, finely chopped
½ cup coarsely chopped red or green
    bell pepper
1 cup sliced mushrooms
1 can (15 oz.) tomato sauce
1 cup dry red wine

1 tsp. dried mixed Italian herbs (or more)
salt and pepper to taste
2 tsp. sugar
½ lb. dried spaghetti, broken into
    2-inch pieces, cooked just 5 minutes
    in salted water
½ cup grated imported Parmesan cheese
1 cup grated sharp cheddar cheese

Preheat oven to 325°. Generously oil two 9-x-5-inch loaf pans. In a large skillet, sauté meat with onion, garlic, pepper and mushrooms. In a large bowl, combine meat mixture with all other ingredients, using just ½ of the cheeses. Transfer to 2 loaf pans and bake for about 40 minutes. Top with remaining cheeses and bake for another 10 minutes until cheeses melt.

# VEGETABLE TORTILLA LASAGNE

*If you are going through the trouble of making lasagne, it's a shame not to make one for another meal. This recipe makes 2 loaves. I don't like to freeze cooked vegetables because I think they lose some of their zing. This lasagne will keep in the refrigerator for a week.*

2½ cups tomato salsa, mild
    or hot
2 tbs. vegetable oil
1 large onion, chopped
3 cloves garlic, finely chopped
1 lb. thin zucchini, cut crosswise into
    ¼-inch slices
½ cup ricotta or small curd cottage
    cheese
1½ cups grated Monterey Jack cheese
½ cup imported Parmesan cheese
1 tsp. ground cumin

1 tsp. chili powder, optional
1 jar (7 oz.) roasted red peppers,
    drained, patted dry and coarsely
    chopped
salt and pepper to taste
2 cups corn kernels, fresh or frozen,
    thawed, uncooked
6 corn tortillas, 6-inch
3-4 tbs. finely chopped fresh cilantro
½ cup grated Monterey Jack cheese
lime wedges for garnish

Preheat oven to 400°. Brush two 9-x-5-inch loaf pans with oil. Put salsa in a fine sieve set over a bowl and drain for 5 minutes. Heat oil in a large skillet. Sauté onion and garlic until just limp. Add zucchini and sauté for 2 minutes. Combine cheeses with cumin and chili powder. Add peppers, salt and pepper to corn.

Layer each loaf pan: 1 tortilla cut to fit pan, ¼ of the sautéed vegetables, ¼ of the cheese mixture, ½ cup corn mixture; ¼ cup salsa, sprinkle of chopped cilantro. Repeat. Top with additional tortilla, a little more salsa and some grated Monterey Jack cheese.

Cover lasagne with aluminum foil and bake for 15 to 20 minutes or until bubbly and cheese is melted. Let stand covered for 5 minutes before serving. Garnish with lime wedges.

# ROASTED VEGETABLE LASAGNE BAKE

*Roasting the vegetables enhances their flavor. This step can be done a day ahead.*
*This recipe fills 2 pans and can be frozen for a couple of weeks.*

¾ lb. eggplant, cut into ¼-inch slices
olive oil
¾ lb. zucchini, cut into ¼-inch slices
1 small red bell pepper, cut into ½-inch slices
1 small yellow bell pepper, cut into ½-inch slices
2 cloves garlic, chopped
1 cup thinly sliced onion
2 cups sliced mushrooms
12 lasagne noodles (about ¾ lb.)
salt and pepper to taste
1 tsp. dried mixed Italian herbs (or less)
1 lb. ricotta cheese
3 cups meatless spaghetti sauce (prepared or homemade)
8 oz. mozzarella cheese, grated

Preheat oven to 425°. Place eggplant slices on a large cookie sheet. Brush both sides of eggplant with a little olive oil and roast until brown on both sides, turning several times with a spatula, about 5 minutes. Watch carefully; it burns easily. Remove eggplant to a large bowl and set aside.

Add a little more olive oil to bowl. Place zucchini, peppers, garlic, onion and mushrooms in oil. Toss to coat. Roast vegetables until lightly browned, turning often. Combine with eggplant.

Cook noodles in a large quantity of boiling salted water for about 5 minutes; they should be undercooked. Drain and sprinkle with a little olive oil to keep from sticking.

Add salt and pepper and Italian herbs to ricotta cheese.

Lower heat to 400°. Divide all ingredients in half, to fit into two pans. Following instructions are for each loaf.

Spread ½ cup sauce in bottom of pan. Layer noodles (use 3), ½ of the ricotta, ½ of the eggplant-vegetable mixture. Spread ½ cup sauce and 3 more noodles. Top with remaining ½ cup sauce. Repeat for second loaf. Cover with foil and bake for about 30 minutes. Uncover, sprinkle with mozzarella and bake for another 15 to 20 minutes until hot and bubbly. Let stand for 5 minutes before serving.

# MUSHROOM-BARLEY LOAF

*The nutty flavor of the barley complements the mushrooms. Cremini or portobello mushrooms have much more flavor than white mushrooms.*

¼ cup butter
1 cup chopped onion
2 cloves garlic, minced
3 cups sliced mushrooms (prefer cremini or portobello)
¾ cup uncooked barley
2 cups beef or chicken stock (or water)
salt and pepper to taste
3 tbs. chopped fresh dill weed or parsley

Preheat oven to 375°. Butter a 9-x-5-inch nonstick loaf pan. Melt butter in a large skillet. Add onion and garlic; cook until onion is wilted. Add mushrooms and barley. Cook for an additional 5 minutes, stirring often, until barley begins to brown. Stir in stock, salt and pepper, and transfer to prepared loaf pan. Bake for 45 to 60 minutes. Remove from oven. Let stand for 5 minutes. Top with dill or parsley.

# CURRIED BULGUR AND LENTIL BAKE

*This Middle Eastern dish is a vegetarian entrée or a satisfying side dish.*

1½ cups lentils (prefer red lentils)
1 tsp. salt (or more)
5 cups water
½ cup bulgur wheat
1 cup boiling water
1 tbs. olive oil
1 medium onion, chopped
1 clove garlic, minced
1 egg, lightly beaten

1 cup chopped drained canned tomatoes
1 jar (4 oz.) chopped jalapeño peppers,
   optional
1 tbs. curry powder (or more)
1 tsp. ground cumin
salt and pepper to taste
3 tbs. chopped fresh cilantro
1 large tomato, chopped, optional

Preheat oven to 350°. Oil a nonstick 9-x-5-inch loaf pan. In a large saucepan, combine lentils and salted water. Bring to boil. Boil for a few minutes. Cover, reduce heat and simmer for about 45 minutes, until lentils are tender. Add more water, if needed. Most of the water will evaporate during cooking.

While lentils are cooking, pour boiling water over bulgur. Let stand for about 10 minutes, until water has been absorbed. Fluff with a fork. Heat olive oil in a skillet. Add onion and garlic and sauté until softened. Combine lentils, bulgur and onion mixture with all other ingredients. Spoon into loaf pan and pack lightly. Bake for about 50 minutes, until loaf is firm. Top with chopped cilantro and tomato.

# ZUCCHINI BULGUR PILAF BAKE

*A clay loaf pan makes a particularly attractive presentation. This recipe used to have 1 pound of ground beef in addition to all the other ingredients, but has been lightened to meet today's standards. If you must have meat, sauté ½ lb. lean ground beef along with the green onions, pepper and garlic.*

1 cup bulgur wheat
2 cups boiling water
1 tbs. olive oil
½ cup sliced green onions, including
    some green
½ cup chopped green or red bell
    pepper (or mixed)
2 cloves garlic, finely minced
½ lb. lean ground lean beef, optional
1 can (1 lb.) tomatoes, cut into pieces,
    with juice
1 lb. zucchini, in ¼-inch slices
1 tbs. Worcestershire sauce
1 tsp. dried oregano
salt and pepper to taste

2 tbs. fresh dill weed, or 1 tsp. dried
1 tsp. sugar
several drops Tabasco Sauce
½ cup shredded sharp cheddar cheese

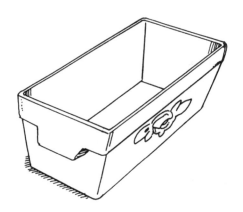

Preheat oven to 350°. Generously oil a loaf pan. Pour boiling water over bulgur. Let stand for about 10 minutes, until water has been absorbed.

Heat oil in a skillet, Sauté onions, pepper, garlic and beef (if using) for a few minutes. Remove to a large bowl. Add drained bulgur wheat, tomatoes and juice, and remaining ingredients, except cheese. Transfer to loaf pan. Cover with aluminum foil and bake for 45 minutes. If the mixture seems too dry, pour ½ cup water or beef stock on top. Sprinkle with cheese. Uncover and bake for another 10 minutes. Let stand a few minutes before serving.

# BULGUR CHEESE BAKE

*This is a vegetarian main dish with an interesting combination of flavors and textures.*

2 cups boiling water
2 tsp. salt
1 cup uncooked bulgur wheat
2 tbs. butter
1 tbs. vegetable oil
1 large onion, chopped
2 cups sliced fresh mushrooms (prefer portobello)
1 red or green bell pepper, chopped

2 tbs. soy sauce
2 tbs. sherry, optional
1/2 tsp. dried mixed Italian herbs
salt and pepper to taste
1 cup cottage cheese
3/4 cup crumbled feta cheese
4 eggs, lightly beaten
paprika

Preheat oven to 350°. Lightly grease a nonstick 9-x-5-inch loaf pan. Pour boiling salted water over bulgur. Let stand for about 10 minutes. Drain well.

In a medium skillet, melt butter; add oil. Sauté onion, mushrooms and pepper until just tender. Remove from heat. Add soy sauce, sherry, herbs, salt and pepper. Combine cottage cheese with feta cheese. Mix well. Spoon bulgur into pan. Cover with vegetables. Place cheese mixture on top. Pour beaten eggs on top. Tap loaf pan on a flat surface to make egg mixture go into bulgur portion of dish. Bake for 45 minutes, until eggs set. Sprinkle with paprika. Let stand for a few minutes before serving.

# BROWN RICE AND PEAS

*This unusual combination is simple to prepare if you have already cooked the brown rice, which can be done the day before.*

1 tbs. butter
2 shallots, minced
1 clove garlic, minced, optional
2 lb. fresh peas (about 2 cups), or 1 pkg.
　(10 oz.) frozen peas, slightly thawed
1/4 cup heavy cream

1 cup chicken stock (prefer homemade)
2 tbs. chopped fresh dill weed or mint
salt and pepper to taste
4 cups cooked brown rice (more or less)
2 tsp. chopped fresh chives

Preheat oven to 350°. Lightly oil a 9-x-5-inch loaf pan. In a medium skillet, melt butter and sauté shallots and garlic until translucent, about 1 minute. Stir in peas. Cook, covered, until just tender, about 8 minutes for fresh peas or 1 minute for frozen. Place 1/2 of the pea mixture in a food processor bowl or blender. Add cream and stock. Process until pureed. Combine pureed mixture with remaining 1/2 of the pea mixture, dill, salt, pepper and cooked rice. Mix well. Transfer to prepared loaf pan and bake, loosely covered, for 15 minutes. Sprinkle with fresh chives and serve.

# SPINACH RICE BAKE

*This side dish, combining rice and vegetable, pairs very well with any meat or poultry. All you need is a salad and you have a complete meal. Use half the can of tomato sauce in the loaf, and the other half in the topping.*

1 tbs. vegetable oil
1 medium onion, chopped
2 cloves garlic, minced
2 pkg. (10 oz. each) frozen chopped spinach,
    thawed and squeezed dry
3 cups cooked rice (can replace 1 cup
    with cooked wild rice)
2 eggs, lightly beaten
1 cup grated Monterey Jack cheese
3/4 cup milk
salt and seasoned pepper to taste
2 tbs. finely chopped fresh basil
1/2 can (8 oz.) tomato sauce (prefer seasoned)

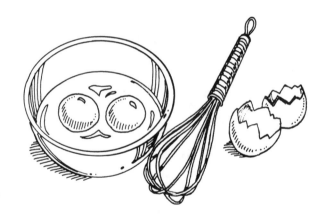

**TOPPING**
1 tsp. dried mixed Italian herbs
½ can (8 oz.) tomato sauce
½ cup grated Parmesan cheese

Preheat oven to 350°. Oil a loaf pan. Heat oil in a skillet. Sauté onion and garlic until limp; add spinach and stir until mixed. Remove to a large bowl. Add rice, eggs, Jack cheese, milk, salt, pepper, basil and tomato sauce. Mix well. Transfer to loaf pan and bake for about 40 minutes. For topping, combine Italian herbs with tomato sauce and Parmesan cheese. Top loaf and return to oven for another 10 minutes.

# PATÉS, TERRINES, MOLDED SALADS AND OTHER COLD LOAVES

# CLAM CHEESE LOG

*This appetizer looks very festive — just right for a holiday table. The flavor improves if it is allowed to mellow in the refrigerator for a day. Serve with assorted crackers and party breads.*

2 pkg. (8 oz. each) low fat cream cheese, softened
2 tbs. lemon juice
2 tsp. Dijon mustard
2 tsp. Worcestershire sauce
2 tbs. chopped fresh parsley (prefer flat-leaf Italian-style)
2 tbs. chopped fresh dill weed
1 medium onion, finely chopped
1 jar (6 oz.) sliced pimiento, undrained
3 jars (7 oz. each) minced clams, mostly drained
1 cup finely crushed saltine crackers
½ cup finely chopped walnuts

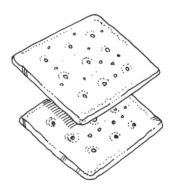

Combine all ingredients except walnuts. Mix well. Pile into a decorative 8-x-4-inch glass loaf pan. Top with walnuts. Chill and serve from loaf pan.

# SEAFOOD TERRINE

*The combination of fish can vary with what is in the market. A mixture of salmon, halibut, haddock, cod or any other firm-fleshed fish works fine. Or use just one fish. Pieces of raw shrimp can substitute for (or add to) scallops. This can be served as part of a buffet, as a first course or as a main dish. It also makes a splendid sandwich filling. You can serve this with an herb mayonnaise.*

2 lb. fish, skinned and boned, in small chunks
¾ cup seasoned breadcrumbs (or more)
½ cup white wine
½ cup half-and-half or whole milk
3 eggs, lightly beaten
2 tsp. prepared horseradish, optional
2 tbs. lemon juice
1 onion, finely chopped
1 tbs. minced chives (prefer fresh)
2 tbs. chopped fresh parsley (prefer flat-leaf Italian-style)
2 tbs. chopped fresh dill weed, or 2 tsp. dried
salt and white pepper to taste
6 oz. sea scallops, cut into small pieces, or shrimp
raw spinach leaves

Preheat oven to 350°. Place skinned and boned fish in a blender or food processor bowl. Process until coarsely chopped. Combine fish with all ingredients, except scallops and spinach leaves. Spoon into a 9-x-5-inch nonstick loaf pan. Push pieces of scallops (or shrimp) into loaf, distributing them evenly. Place loaf pan in a large baking pan. Add enough hot water to baking pan to come halfway up the sides of the loaf pan. Bake for about 30 minutes until fish is done. Let cool in pan for 10 minutes. Drain off any liquid and chill for 1 to 2 hours. Turn out onto a platter lined with raw spinach leaves.

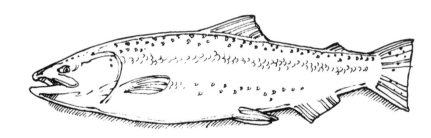

# TURKEY-VEGETABLE TERRINE

*This is one of those indestructible recipes. Add or subtract ingredients or change the proportions. The colors are lovely. Anything you do just seems to make it better. Spooned into a pita bread pocket, it makes a delicious sandwich filling.*

⅓ cup chopped onion
1 clove garlic, chopped
1 lb. lean ground turkey
1 egg, lightly beaten
¼ cup seasoned breadcrumbs
1 tart apple, coarsely grated (prefer Granny Smith)
1 cup chopped celery
1 cup grated carrots
1 cup frozen peas, thawed
½ cup diced red bell pepper
1 tbs. Dijon mustard
1 tbs. Worcestershire sauce
2 tbs. finely chopped fresh basil, or 1 tsp. dried
2 tbs. chopped fresh parsley
salt and pepper to taste

Preheat oven to 350° Lightly oil a nonstick loaf pan. In a large bowl, combine all ingredients. Spoon mixture into a loaf pan. Cover with aluminum foil and place in a large baking pan. Add enough hot water to baking pan to come halfway up sides of loaf pan. Bake for about 30 minutes. Remove foil cover and continue to bake for another 30 minutes, until done. Remove from oven. Pour off excess liquid and cool. Refrigerate for several hours before serving. Unmold onto a platter.

# ITALIAN TURKEY LOAF

*This moist loaf is a hearty main course that can be eaten cold or hot. Italian sausage adds a special flavor to this dish, but you can use less (or omit it), if you like.*

1½ lb. lean ground turkey
½ lb. hot Italian turkey sausage, casing removed
1 cup tomato sauce
¾ cup Italian-seasoned breadcrumbs
1 cup chopped portobello mushrooms
½ cup coarsely chopped red bell pepper
2 cloves garlic, minced
1 medium onion, coarsely chopped

¾ cup shredded mozzarella cheese
½ cup grated imported Parmesan cheese
2 tbs. chopped fresh basil, or 1 tsp. dried
2 tbs. chopped fresh parsley (prefer flat-leaf Italian-style)
salt and pepper to taste
additional cheese for garnish, optional

Preheat oven to 350°. If using sausage, use a loaf pan with a trivet to catch most of the fat. In a large bowl, combine all ingredients. Mix well. Transfer mixture to loaf pan. Bake for about 1¼ hours, until done. Let cool to room temperature before chilling in the refrigerator. If serving warm, let stand for 5 minutes after it is removed from the oven before cutting.

# CHICKEN LIVER PATÉ WITH COGNAC

*This simple-to-fix paté is a special treat. Serve with rye or pumpernickel bread.*

½ cup butter, softened
2 medium onions, chopped
1½ lb. chicken livers
½ tsp. dried marjoram
½ tsp. dried savory
2 tsp. dried tarragon
salt and pepper to taste
2-3 jiggers cognac
1 cup sliced red radish

In a medium skillet, melt butter. Sauté onions until limp; add chicken livers and cook for a few minutes. Do not overcook; livers should still be pink on the inside. Add all seasonings. Mix well. Add cognac and mix again. Add a little more butter if mixture seems too stiff. Put liver mixture in the food processor bowl and process until very smooth. Pile into a pretty glass 8-x-4-inch loaf pan. Top with red radish slices; chill for a few hours before serving.

# MEDITERRANEAN VEGETABLE TERRINE

*The colors are vivid, and the flavors are robust. This terrine can be a first course with a crusty bread or used as a side dish to accompany a roast.*

1 eggplant, 1 lb., peeled in strips and
    thinly sliced
1 lb. zucchini (thin, if possible), thinly
    sliced
kosher salt
1 large red bell pepper, cut in half,
    seeds removed
1 large yellow bell pepper, cut in half,
    seeds removed
1 tbs. olive oil

2 tbs. olive oil
1 onion, thinly sliced
4 large cloves garlic, minced
salt and white pepper to taste
1 tsp. dried mixed Italian herbs
1 tbs. chopped fresh basil, or 1 tsp.
    dried (or pesto, if available)
4 oz. goat (chèvre) cheese, plain or
    herbed
1/4 cup minced fresh parsley

Place eggplant and zucchini slices in a colander. Sprinkle with salt and cover with a plate with a weight on top (a filled tea kettle works fine). Let drain (in the sink) for at least 1 hour. Rinse well and dry with paper towels.

Preheat broiler. Place peppers skin side up on a foil-lined cookie sheet (to help with cleanup). Sprinkle with 1 tbs. olive oil and broil until skins are blackened, about 5 minutes, turning so that all sides broil. Watch them; you want them blackened, not charred. Remove peppers to a small paper bag and let them steam for a few minutes; it makes skins easier to remove. When cool enough to handle, remove skins and discard. It doesn't matter if some of the skins do not come off. Cut peppers into thick slices. Set aside.

In a large skillet, heat 2 tbs. oil; toss with onion and garlic. Cook until soft, about 5 minutes. Add eggplant, zucchini, salt, pepper and herbs. Cook for 8 to 10 minutes until vegetables are tender, not mushy.

Reduce oven heat to 300°. Oil a 9-x-5-inch nonstick loaf pan with a trivet, or line a regular loaf pan with aluminum foil. Layer ⅔ of the eggplant-zucchini mixture, red and yellow peppers, basil leaves and remaining ⅓ of the eggplant-zucchini mixture. Cover pan with aluminium foil. Place covered terrine in a larger pan filled with hot water that reaches halfway up sides of loaf pan. Bake for 1 hour. Remove terrine from oven and cool to room temperature. Place a weight on top of foil and refrigerate for 24 hours. Unmold.

To serve, top with chèvre. It is a nice touch to run the terrine under the broiler for a few minutes to melt the chèvre. Sprinkle with fresh parsley.

# SPINACH AND FETA TORTE

*An absolutely knock-your-socks-off dish. It is a spectacular starter or a splendid lunch or a special brunch. Squeeze the spinach very dry. Use the best feta cheese you can find; in this dish, it does make a difference. Use a clay pan, if you have one. It makes a beautiful crust.*

½ cup unsalted butter
1 large onion, minced
3 cloves garlic, minced
4 pkg. (10 oz. each) frozen chopped
　　spinach, thawed and squeezed dry
2 eggs, lightly beaten
¼ lb. feta cheese, crumbled
½ cup grated imported Parmesan cheese
3 tbs. chopped fresh dill
salt and pepper to taste

¼ cup minced fresh parsley (prefer flat-
　　leaf Italian-style)
½ tsp. nutmeg (prefer freshly grated)
8 sheets phyllo dough, thawed,
　　following package directions
6 tbs. butter, melted and cooled  (or
　　more)
3 hard-cooked eggs, cooled and peeled
lemon wedges

Preheat oven to 375°. Butter a 9-x-5-inch loaf pan. Melt butter in a skillet. Sauté onion and garlic until translucent. Add spinach to onion and garlic. Cook mixture over moderate heat, stirring until all liquid is evaporated.

In a food processor bowl or blender, puree mixture with 2 eggs. Remove to a large bowl and combine pureed mixture with feta and Parmesan cheeses and seasonings. Mix well.

With phyllo dough, speed counts; the dough dries very quickly. Stack sheets between lightly dampened dish towels. Remove one sheet at a time. Lay it on a sheet of waxed paper and butter it with a pastry brush. Continue to butter and layer sheets of phyllo one on top of the other until 6 sheets have been used; keep remaining sheets between towels. Working quickly, fit buttered sheets crosswise into loaf pan, letting edges hang over long sides of pan. Cut remaining 2 phyllo sheets in half, lengthwise, butter and stack them and fit them into pan so that edges hang over short sides of pan.

Spread ½ of the spinach filling over phyllo; arrange eggs lengthwise down the center. Spread remaining filling over eggs, packing as tightly as possible. Fold overhanging phyllo over filling to enclose completely. Brush with remaining melted butter.

Bake torte in middle of oven for about 1 hour or a bit more until top is golden. Let cool in pan, on a rack, for 10 minutes, invert a platter on top and unmold. Let cool to room temperature before slicing. Serve with lemon wedges. Serve thin slices or people won't eat anything else.

# SPINACH CARROT TERRINE

*This makes a lovely presentation, offering different colors and textures. It can be served cold as an appetizer. Served warm, it is an elegant addition to a dinner plate. It keeps well in the refrigerator for several days. It is not on anyone's reducing diet.*

grated Parmesan cheese for sprinkling pan

### SPINACH MIXTURE
3 pkg. (10 oz. each) frozen spinach, thawed
1 pkg. (8 oz.) cream cheese, softened
3 eggs, lightly beaten
2 tbs. flour (or more)
1 large shallot, finely chopped
1 tsp. dried dill weed
1 tsp. dried mixed Italian herbs (or less), optional
salt and white pepper to taste
¾ cup shredded cheddar cheese

## CARRROT MIXTURE

1½ cups shredded raw carrots
2 eggs, lightly beaten
1 large shallot, finely chopped
1 tsp. ground ginger
salt and white pepper to taste
2 tbs. flour (or more)
½ cup shredded Monterey Jack cheese or Swiss cheese
1 tbs. plain yogurt
flat-leaf parsley or watercress leaves for garnish, optional

Preheat oven to 350°. Butter a 9-x-5-inch loaf pan. Sprinkle buttered pan with Parmesan cheese, tapping pan to distribute cheese evenly.

In one bowl, combine spinach mixture ingredients. In another bowl, combine carrot mixture ingredients. Place ½ of the spinach mixture in prepared loaf pan; spoon on carrot mixture, smoothing top. Finish with remaining ½ of the spinach mixture. Bake for 45 minutes, until slightly puffed. Let cool and unmold. Garnish.

# WHITE BEAN AND SUN-DRIED TOMATO PATÉ

*Served in an attractive small clay loaf pan, this makes a classy appetizer.*
Accompany with cocktail rye bread or crispbread.

1 tbs. vegetable oil
1 large onion, chopped
2 cloves garlic, minced
2 cups canned cannellini beans, rinsed and drained
½ cup oil-cured sun-dried tomatoes, well drained
2 tbs. lemon juice
2 tbs. chopped fresh parsley (prefer flat-leaf Italian-syle)
½ tsp. dried thyme
½ tsp. savory
salt and pepper to taste
2 tbs. water

In a small skillet, heat oil. Sauté onion and garlic until onion is just beginning to brown. Remove from heat and set aside. Combine all ingredients, including sautéed onion, in the bowl of a food processor and process until very smooth. Stop and scrape down sides as needed. Pat into a small loaf pan (clay) and serve warm or cold.

# MOLDED RICE SALAD

*A molded salad makes a festive presentation. This one goes with anything and is a nice addition to a buffet.*

1/2 cup slivered almonds
6 cups hot cooked rice (2 cups raw)
1/2 cup mayonnaise
1/3 cup sliced pitted black olives
1/3 cup sliced pimiento-stuffed green olives
1/4 cup chopped green onions
2 tbs. chopped fresh parsley
2 tbs. chopped fresh basil, or 1 tsp. dried
2 tbs. fresh lemon juice
salt and pepper to taste
cherry tomatoes and radishes for garnish

Oil a 9-x-5-inch glass loaf pan. Toast almonds in oven or microwave. Toss with hot cooked rice and all other ingredients. Pack into loaf pan and chill for several hours. Invert onto a serving platter and garnish.

# CHICKEN PESTO SALAD LOAF

*When it's your turn to bring the salad to a potluck, this is a good recipe to have on hand. It can easily be doubled (one loaf for each end of the table). Use a glass loaf pan with a fitted plastic lid for transporting.*

1 cup cubed zucchini, ½-inch cubes
1 cup thinly sliced carrots
½ cup sliced green onions, including some green
1 tbs. vegetable oil
3-4 cups finely chopped cooked chicken
½ lb. rotini (mixed colors: spinach, tomato, egg), cooked according to package directions
½ cup diced tomatoes
½ cup chopped celery
⅓ cup sour cream

⅓ cup mayonnaise
2 tbs. lemon juice
2 tbs. olive oil
3 tbs. chopped fresh basil
2 cloves garlic, chopped
2 tbs. chopped fresh parsley (prefer flat-leaf Italian-style)
1 tsp. dried mixed Italian herbs
salt and pepper to taste
½ cup toasted pine nuts

Sauté zucchini, carrots and onions in oil until vegetables are tender-crisp. In a large bowl, combine chicken with cooked pasta and sautéed vegetables, tomatoes, celery, sour cream and mayonnaise.

For the pesto: Place lemon juice and all the other ingredients in a blender or food processor bowl. Process until mixture is the consistency of a coarse paste. Toss with chicken noodle mixture. Pile into a loaf pan and top with additional pine nuts. Chill for several hours before serving from the loaf pan.

# LOAVES OF BREAD: QUICK AND YEASTED

# CREAM OF CORN BREAD

*This makes a dense and moist bread. You can substitute 1 percent milk for regular milk, and margarine for the butter. It won't taste exactly the same, but it will lower the calories.*

1⅓ cups yellow cornmeal
1⅓ cups flour
½ cup sugar (or less)
1 tbs. baking powder
1 tsp. salt
3 eggs

1 can (1 lb.) cream-style corn, slightly drained
1 cup milk
⅓ cup butter, melted
1 tsp. dried dill weed, optional

Preheat oven to 375°. Butter a 9-x-5-inch loaf pan. In a large bowl, combine dry ingredients. In a medium bowl, beat eggs. Stir in corn, milk and butter, and mix until completely combined. Stir liquid ingredients into dry ingredients. Add dill. Mix until just blended (do not overmix). Pour into prepared loaf pan. Bake for 40 to 50 minutes until a toothpick inserted into the center comes out clean. Cool on a rack. Remove from pan.

# CORNBREAD LOAF

*This bread is similar to a traditional skillet cornbread. The corn kernels give it an added crunch. It goes with any Southwestern meal and most salads. It can be frozen for several weeks.*

cornmeal for dusting pan
1½ cups flour
1¼ cups yellow cornmeal
1 tbs. sugar
1 tsp. baking powder
1 tsp. baking soda
2 tsp. salt
3 eggs, lightly beaten
⅓ cup light oil (peanut or canola)
1 cup buttermilk or sour milk (made by
    adding 1 tbs. lemon juice or white vinegar
    to 1 cup milk and letting the mixture stand
    for about 10 minutes)
1 cup corn kernels, fresh or frozen, uncooked
1 tbs. fresh thyme, or 1 tsp. dried

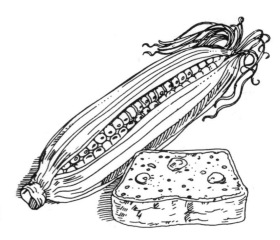

Preheat oven to 350°. Oil a loaf pan and dust with cornmeal. In a large bowl, stir together flour, cornmeal, sugar, baking powder, baking soda and salt. In another bowl, mix together eggs, oil, buttermilk, corn kernels and thyme. Stir liquid mixture into dry mixture until just combined. Pour into prepared pan. Bake for 15 minutes. Reduce heat to 325° and continue baking for about 50 minutes, until a toothpick inserted into the center comes out clean. Remove pan to a wire rack for 5 minutes. Turn out onto rack for 20 minutes before slicing.

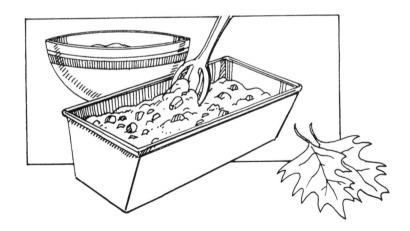

# OLD-FASHIONED CORNBREAD

*This loaf can be a last-minute decision. The recipe is so simple, it can be easily memorized. For the most part, it is one of everything. A clay pan makes a gorgeous crust.*

1 cup flour
1 cup yellow cornmeal
½ cup sugar (or a little less)
1 tsp. baking powder
1 tsp. baking soda
1 tsp. salt
2 tbs. butter or margarine, melted, or oil

1 egg, lightly beaten
1 cup sour milk (made by adding 2 tbs. vinegar to 1 cup milk and letting it stand for 10 minutes)
kernels from 1 ear corn, cooked or uncooked, optional
1 tbs. finely chopped fresh dill, optional

Preheat oven to 375°. Generously grease a loaf pan. Place dry ingredients in a bowl. Add liquid ingredients, corn and dill. Mix until just moistened. Turn into loaf pan and bake for about 45 minutes until a toothpick inserted in the center comes out clean. Let cool in pan for about 10 minutes. Turn out onto a rack. Serve warm or cold.

# HERB-CHEESE BREAD

*This simple bread, made with baking powder, seems to go well with just about everything. It is a welcome addition to a buffet.*

2¼ cups whole wheat pastry flour
2½ tsp. baking powder
½ tsp. salt
¾ tsp. dried dill weed
¾ tsp. dried basil
½ tsp. dried thyme
½ tsp. dried savory

2 eggs, lightly beaten
2 tbs. honey
½ cup milk
¼ cup vegetable oil
1 cup grated sharp cheddar or Monterey Jack cheese

Preheat oven to 350°. Oil and flour a nonstick 9-x-5-inch loaf pan. In a large bowl, combine dry ingredients and herbs. Stir until mixed. In a separate bowl, combine all other ingredients, except cheese. Add wet ingredients to dry ingredients, a little at a time. Stir with a wooden spoon until well blended. Add cheese and stir until it is evenly distributed in dough. Transfer dough to prepared loaf pan and bake for 50 minutes, until top is brown and a toothpick inserted into the center comes out clean.

Remove to a wire rack. Cool for 5 minutes. Remove bread from pan and finish cooling completely on rack.

# ONION RYE BREAD

*This tasty bread goes very well with hearty soups or salads. Use a little more onion, if you like a stronger onion flavor.*

1½ cups rye flour
1 cup unbleached white flour
3 tbs. wheat germ
2 tbs. brown sugar
1 tsp. salt
2½ tsp. baking powder

1 egg, beaten
1 cup buttermilk or plain low fat yogurt
3 tbs. vegetable oil
1 small onion, finely chopped
1 tsp. caraway or poppy seeds for
    topping, optional

Preheat oven to 350°. Lightly oil and flour a nonstick 9-x-5-inch loaf pan. In a large bowl, combine dry ingredients. In a separate bowl, combine egg and buttermilk; stir until smooth. In a small skillet, heat oil; sauté onion over low heat, until golden. Cool for a few minutes, and stir into egg mixture. Add wet ingredients to dry ingredients, a little at a time. With a wooden spoon, stir well until ingredients are well blended and a sticky dough forms. Transfer dough into prepared loaf pan. Sprinkle top with seeds, if desired. Bake for 50 to 55 minutes, until top is golden and a toothpick inserted into the center comes out clean. Remove pan to a rack. Cool for 10 minutes. Turn out bread on rack to cool completely.

# IRISH SODA BREAD

*This recipe makes 2 dense tasty loaves. Tightly wrapped, the loaves will keep for a few days at room temperature. Do not refrigerate; it tends to dry the bread. It can be frozen for a few weeks.*

3 cups multigrain flour (available in health food stores)
1 cup whole wheat flour
2 tbs. sugar (can use brown sugar)
3 tsp. baking powder
1½ tsp. baking soda
1 tsp. salt

6 tbs. butter, well chilled and cut into small pieces
1¾ cups (or slightly more) buttermilk or plain low fat yogurt
1 egg, beaten
2 tbs. caraway seeds
½ cup raisins

Preheat oven to 350°, with rack in the middle of the oven. Butter two 9-x-5-inch loaf pans. In a large bowl, mix dry ingredients. With a pastry blender or 2 knives, cut in butter until mixture resembles coarse crumbs (or do this in a food processor and transfer to bowl). Add buttermilk and egg. Mix for about 1 minute, adding caraway seeds and raisins as you mix. Add a little more buttermilk, if needed, to get a soft dough. Place dough into prepared pans and bake on center rack for about 45 minutes. Bread should be brown and crusty. Cool loaves on a rack.

# SWEET POTATO SPICE BREAD

*This recipe makes two 9-x-5-inch loaves. If you have small pans, you can divide the batter among 5 or 6 pans (depending on size). The aroma of spice in the kitchen, while the breads are baking, makes it a real test of self-control to allow them to mellow before devouring them. Use clay pans if you have them.*

4 cups unbleached flour
2 tsp. baking soda
1/2 tsp. baking powder
1 tsp. salt
1 1/2 tsp. cinnamon
1/2 tsp. ground ginger
1/2 tsp. allspice
1/2 tsp. nutmeg
1/4 tsp. ground cloves

1 cup chopped walnuts
1/2 cup dried, but moist, currants
2/3 cup margarine, softened
1 1/2 cups sugar
4 eggs, room temperature
1 cup light molasses
2 tsp. vanilla extract
2 1/2 cups pureed cooked sweet potatoes

Preheat oven to 350°. Lightly butter and flour two 9-x-5-inch loaf pans.

Onto a piece of waxed paper, sift together flour, baking soda, baking powder and spices. Set aside.

In a small bowl, combine walnuts and currants. Add 1 tbs. of the sifted flour mixture. Set aside.

In a large bowl, with an electric mixer at medium speed, cream shortening until light, about 3 minutes. Add 1/2 of the sugar; cream well. Add remaining sugar; cream well. Add eggs one at a time, beating well after each addition. On low speed, blend in molasses and vanilla. Scrape down sides of bowl. Add 1/2 of the flour mixture, and beat just until flour has been absorbed; do not overbeat. Add pureed sweet potatoes, beat until incorporated, and then add remaining flour mixture. Stir in walnuts and currants.

Divide batter between prepared loaf pans. Bake on middle rack of oven for about 1 hour, until a toothpick inserted into the center comes out clean. Cool loaves in pan on a wire rack for 10 minutes. Turn out on rack to finish cooling. Let loaves mature for a day before using. Store loaves airtight.

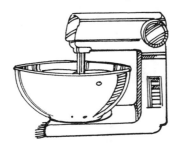

# ZUCCHINI APRICOT SWEET BREAD

*This bread is perfect for brunch or dessert. It is moist and spicy and not too sweet. It can be topped with a dollop of whipped cream, but it really isn't necessary. Dried peaches or pears can be substituted for apricots.*

½ cup vegetable oil (prefer canola)
4 eggs, lightly beaten
½ cup light brown sugar, firmly packed
¼ cup milk
2 tsp. vanilla extract
2 cups (about ½ lb.) grated zucchini (do not peel unless skin is tough)
1 tbs. grated orange peel
1 cup whole wheat flour
1 cup white unbleached flour

2 tsp. baking powder
1 tsp. baking soda
2 tsp. cinnamon
1 tsp. nutmeg
1 tsp. ground cloves
½ tsp. allspice
½ tsp. salt
¾ cup chopped dried apricots
¾ cup chopped walnuts or pecans

Preheat oven to 350°. Generously oil loaf pan. In a large bowl, beat together oil, eggs, sugar, milk and vanilla. Add zucchini and orange peel.

Sift together dry ingredients into a medium bowl. Stir dry ingredients into liquid ingredients, and mix until just combined. Fold in apricots and nuts. Spread in prepared loaf pan. Bake for about 1 hour and 15 minutes in middle of oven, or until a toothpick inserted into the center comes out clean.

Cool for 10 minutes in pan. Turn out on a rack and cool completely. Wrap in foil and let stand overnight to develop flavors.

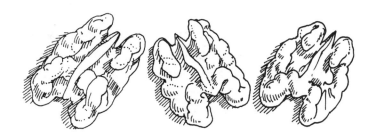

# BROWN BREAD

*This is as close as you can get to an authentic Boston brown bread. It is a most satisfying accompaniment to baked beans or eaten just by itself. Note that there are no eggs in this loaf, but it is filled with plenty of good things.*

1 cup white flour
2 cups whole wheat flour
2 tsp. baking soda
1 tsp. salt
½ tsp. ground ginger, optional
½ cup dark brown sugar, firmly packed
½ cup dark molasses

2 cups buttermilk or sour milk (made by combining 1¾ cups milk with ¼ cup white vinegar and letting the mixture stand for 5 minutes)
1 cup dark raisins
¾ cup coarsely chopped walnuts

Preheat oven to 350°. Grease and flour a 9-x-5-inch loaf pan. In a large bowl, combine all dry ingredients. Add remaining ingredients and stir until just combined. Pour batter into prepared pan and bake for about 1 hour, or until a toothpick inserted into the center comes out clean. Let bread stand in pan on a rack for about 5 minutes. Turn loaf out on rack and cool completely before slicing.

# FRUIT BREAD

*This cake-like bread is made from simple pantry items. It is moist and delectable. Other dried fruits may be used as well.*

1½ cups boiling water
1 cup Grape Nuts (not flakes)
1 cup chopped dates, prunes or raisins (or combination)
1 egg, lightly beaten
2 tsp. baking soda
2 tbs. butter or margarine, melted
¾ cup sugar
1½ cups flour
1 tsp. salt
½ cup chopped walnuts, optional

Preheat oven to 350°. Lightly grease a nonstick loaf pan. Pour boiling water over Grape Nuts and fruits. Let stand for 20 minutes. Drain excess water (if there is any). Combine fruit and Grape Nuts with all other ingredients. Mix well. Place in prepared pan and bake for about 1 hour, or until a toothpick inserted into the center comes out clean. Let stand in pan for 10 minutes. Remove from pan to a large cake platter.

# CARROT BANANA BREAD

*This is a very appealing combination, a bread made from ordinary ingredients. Children who wouldn't touch a carrot will gobble this up. Use a food processor to shred the carrots.*

1/2 cup butter or margarine, softened
1 cup brown sugar, firmly packed
2 eggs, lightly beaten
2 cups flour
1 tsp. baking soda
1/2 tsp. baking powder
1 tsp. cinnamon

1/2 tsp. nutmeg
1/2 tsp. salt
1 cup mashed bananas, leaving some
   lumps
1 cup shredded carrots
1/2 cup coarsely chopped nuts

Preheat oven to 350°. Butter a loaf pan. In a large bowl, cream together butter and sugar. Beat in eggs. Combine dry ingredients. Blend into butter-sugar mixture alternately with bananas. Add carrots and nuts. Pour into prepared pan. Bake for about 50 minutes, or until a toothpick inserted into the center comes out clean. Cool for 10 minutes in pan. Turn out of pan on a rack and cool completely.

# BANANA SURPRISE BREAD

*The "surprise" makes this more a cake than a bread. It makes a lovely, easy-to-manage dessert. A bit of vanilla ice cream on top never hurts.*

1¾ cups flour
1 tbs. baking powder
½ tsp. salt
¾ cup sugar
½ cup margarine, softened
1 tsp. vanilla extract
2 eggs, lightly beaten
1 cup mashed bananas
½ cup chocolate chips (or more)
½ cup coarsely chopped walnuts

Preheat oven to 350°. Grease a loaf pan. Mix together flour, baking powder and salt. In another large bowl, beat together sugar, margarine, vanilla and eggs. Mix in bananas. Add flour mixture and stir until just smooth; do not overbeat. Add chocolate chips and nuts. Pour into prepared pan, making sides of loaf a little higher than center. Bake for 50 to 60 minutes, until a toothpick inserted into the center comes out clean. Let stand for 10 minutes. Remove from pan and cool completely on a rack.

# BANANA WALNUT LOAF

*There are a million recipes for banana bread. This one is a moist and tasty. It cuts beautifully and keeps forever in the freezer.*

1/3 cup butter or margarine, softened
3/4 cup sugar
2 eggs, lightly beaten
2 cups flour
1/2 tsp. salt
1/2 tsp. baking soda
1 tsp. cinnamon
1 1/2 cups coarsely chopped overripe bananas (about 3 large bananas), leaving
    some lumps
1/2 cup coarsely chopped walnuts

Preheat oven to 350°. Grease a 9-x-5-inch loaf pan. Combine all ingredients. Mix thoroughly. Pour into prepared pan, making sides of loaf higher than middle. Let stand for about 20 minutes. Bake for 1 hour, or until a toothpick inserted into the center comes out clean. Let cool on rack. Remove from pan.

# ALMOND TEA BREAD

*The addition of toasted slivered almonds makes this bread more like a cake. Spread with butter, and placed under the broiler, it tastes even better. It is a perfect accompaniment to an afternoon cup of tea or coffee.*

½ cup butter, softened
¾ cup sugar
½ tsp. almond extract
1 egg, lightly beaten
½ tsp. almond extract
2 cups flour

½ tsp. baking powder
¼ tsp. baking soda
¼ tsp. salt
½ cup half-and-half
½ cup slivered almonds, lightly toasted

Preheat oven to 325°. Butter a loaf pan. Cream butter with sugar until thoroughly mixed. Add egg and almond extract and mix until well blended. Sift flour with baking powder, baking soda and salt. Add flour mixture alternately with half-and-half to creamed mixture, mixing until well blended. Stir in almonds. Pour into prepared loaf pan. Bake for 60 to 70 minutes, or until a toothpick inserted into the center comes out clean. Cool in pan for a few minutes. Turn out on a wire rack to continue cooling.

# PEAR QUICK BREAD

*For best flavor, this bread should "age" for a day before serving. It will keep in the freezer for a few months. Ginger adds a nice bite, but can be omitted. This recipe makes two 9-x-5-inch loaves. If you have smaller pans, the batter can be divided into 3 parts.*

4 ripe Bartlett pears
4 cups flour
1½ tsp. baking powder
½ tsp. baking soda
½ tsp. salt
2 tsp. ground ginger, optional (more or less)
1½ cups sugar
½ cup vegetable oil
½ cup butter or margarine, melted
1 tbs. grated lemon peel (or less)
2 tsp. vanilla extract
4 eggs
½ cup finely chopped dried pears
1 tbs. sugar

Preheat oven to 350°. Grease two 9-x-5-inch glass loaf pans. Peel and core pears. Set aside 1 pear; dice remaining pears. Combine flour, baking powder, baking soda and salt. In a large bowl, combine ginger, sugar, oil, butter, lemon peel and vanilla. With a wooden spoon, beat until blended. Add eggs, one at a time, beating after each addition. Add fresh diced and dried pears. Beat for 1 minute longer. Add flour mixture and beat until blended; mixture will be thick. Divide batter into 2 pans. Thinly slice remaining pear, and place ½ pear on top of batter in each pan. Sprinkle with 1 tbs. sugar.

Bake for about 1 hour or until a toothpick inserted in the center comes out clean. Place pans on a wire rack and cool for about 15 minutes. Remove from pans and cool completely. Store tightly wrapped.

# ORANGE CRANBERRY BREAD

*Bake an extra loaf when fresh cranberries are plentiful. This bread freezes very well. If using frozen cranberries, do not thaw. It's great for the holidays.*

1½ cups fresh or frozen cranberries
1¼ cups sugar
3 cups flour
2 tsp. baking powder
1 tsp. baking soda
1 tsp. salt
½ tsp. ground cloves
½ tsp. nutmeg
⅓ cup butter or margarine, softened
2 eggs, lightly beaten
2 tsp. grated fresh orange peel
1 cup orange juice
¾ cup light raisins
¾ cup coarsely chopped walnuts

Preheat oven to 350°. Generously grease a 9-x-5-inch loaf pan. In a small bowl, combine cranberries and ¼ cup of the sugar; toss to mix. Coarsely chop in a food processor or blender (or leave whole cranberries if you prefer).

In a large bowl, place remaining 1 cup sugar and all other dry ingredients. Cut in butter with a pastry cutter or 2 knives until crumbly. Stir in eggs, orange peel and orange juice at once. Stir just until evenly moist. Fold in raisins and walnuts; stir in cranberries. Do not overmix. Spoon into prepared pan, making sides of loaf higher than middle. Bake for 1 hour and 10 minutes or until a toothpick inserted into the center comes out clean. Cool for 10 minutes. Transfer from pan to a rack to complete cooling.

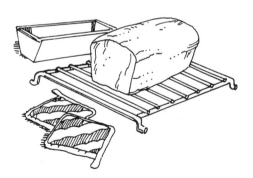

# SESAME BUTTERSCOTCH BREAD

*The addition of sesame seeds to the topping adds to the appeal of this rich satisfying bread.*

2 tbs. sesame seeds
2 tbs. sugar
½ tsp. cinnamon
½ tsp. nutmeg
2 cups flour
1 tsp. baking powder
½ tsp. baking soda
1 tsp. salt

2 eggs, lightly beaten
1 cup brown sugar
3 tbs. butter or margarine, melted
1 cup buttermilk or sour milk (made by adding 2 tbs. white vinegar to 1 cup of milk and letting it stand 5 minutes)
⅔ cup coarsely chopped hazelnuts or walnuts

Preheat oven to 350°. Generously grease a 9-x-5-inch loaf pan. Combine sesame seeds with sugar, cinnamon and nutmeg; set aside. Sift together dry ingredients. In a large bowl, combine eggs, brown sugar and melted butter; mix well. Add flour mixture alternately with buttermilk, stirring just until blended; do not overmix. Stir in nuts. Pour into prepared pan, leaving a slight depression in the middle. Sprinkle top with sesame seed mixture. Bake for about 1 hour or until bread starts to pull away from sides of pan. Cool slightly and turn out on a rack. Serve warm or cold.

# LEMON TEA BREAD

*This simple bread makes a satisfying snack. A lemon sherbet topping makes it a special dessert. Add blueberries only when they are fresh. It does not work with frozen berries. This bread tastes better if eaten the following day.*

2 tsp. grated fresh lemon peel
¾ cup sugar
⅓ cup softened butter or margarine (or half of each)
2 eggs, lightly beaten
1½ cups flour

1 tsp. baking powder
½ tsp. salt
½ cup milk
½ cup finely chopped pecans or walnuts
½ cup fresh blueberries, optional

**TOPPING**
½ cup granulated sugar

¼ cup fresh lemon juice

Preheat oven to 325°. Grease and flour an 8-x-4-inch loaf pan. Cream together lemon peel, sugar and butter. Add all other ingredients, except topping, and mix well. Pour batter into prepared pan. Bake for 50 minutes, until a toothpick inserted into the center comes out clean. While bread is baking, mix together sugar and lemon juice. Take bread out of oven and immediately spoon sweetened lemon juice over hot loaf. Cool for a few minutes and turn out on a rack.

# PUMPKIN NUT LOAF

*This bread makes a delicious snack. Spread with cream cheese, it is a special treat.*

¾ cup raisins
⅓ cup water (can use all or part sherry)
2 eggs
½ cup vegetable oil
¼ cup water
1 cup pureed pumpkin (unsweetened)
2 cups flour

¾ cup sugar
1 tsp. baking soda
1 tsp. cinnamon
½ tsp. nutmeg
½ tsp. salt
½ cup coarsely chopped walnuts

Preheat oven to 350°. Oil a 9-x-5-inch loaf pan. Combine raisins and water (or sherry) in a saucepan. Bring to a boil over high heat. Remove from heat and set aside to cool. In a mixing bowl, whisk together eggs, oil, water and pumpkin puree. Stir to combine. In another large bowl, combine dry ingredients. Stir in pumpkin mixture, undrained raisins and walnuts. Transfer batter to prepared loaf pan. Bake until a toothpick inserted into the center comes out clean, 1 to 1½ hours. Cool on a rack.

# SPICED PUMPKIN RAISIN BREAD

*This recipe makes 2 breads, just right for holiday time. The bread freezes very well, so it can be baked weeks in advance.*

2/3 cup butter or margarine, softened
  (do not use oil)
2½ cups sugar
4 eggs
1 can (1 lb.) pureed pumpkin
2/3 cup water
2½ cups flour
1½ cups whole wheat flour

1 tsp. baking powder
2 tsp. baking soda
1½ tsp. salt
1 tsp. ground cloves
2 tsp. cinnamon
1 tsp. ground cardamom
1½ cups raisins

Preheat oven to 350°. Generously grease two 9-x-5-inch loaf pans. In a large bowl, cream together butter with sugar until light and fluffy. Beat in eggs until well blended. Stir in pumpkin and water, mixing well. Sift together dry ingredients, mixing until just blended. Add raisins. Divide batter evenly between prepared pans. Bake until loaves are browned and a toothpick inserted into the center comes out clean, about 1¼ hours. Let loaves cool in pans on a rack.

# OATMEAL BREAD

*This is a good addition to anyone's collection. Simple to make from pantry ingredients, it is tasty and nutritious. This recipe makes 2 loaves.*

2 cups hot water
1 cup old-fashioned rolled oats (do not use instant)
$1/4$ cup sugar
$1/4$ cup dark brown sugar or honey
2 tbs. butter or margarine
$1\frac{1}{2}$ tsp. salt
$1/2$ cup warm water (about 110°)
1 pkg. active dry yeast
5-6 cups flour, plus flour for the board

In a large bowl, combine hot water, oats, sugars, butter and salt. Stir well and let stand until cool.

Pour warm water into a glass bowl. Sprinkle yeast over top and let stand until it foams, about 5 minutes. Add to oat mixture. Add 5 cups flour and mix to form a dough. Dough should be soft but not sticky. Stir in more flour as needed.

Turn dough onto a floured board and knead until smooth and elastic (about 8 to 10 minutes). Transfer to a greased bowl and let rise in a draft-free place until double in bulk (about 1½ hours). Dough should be soft but not sticky.

Punch down and knead for another minute (to remove air pockets). Divide dough in half, form into a loaf and place in 2 greased 9-x-5-inch loaf pans. Cover loosely and let rise until doubled in bulk, about 1 hour.

When loaves have almost doubled, heat oven to 375°. When loaves have doubled, bake for about 45 minutes, until brown. Loaves should sound hollow when tapped. Invert on a rack to cool completely.

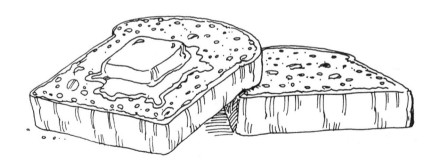

# SWEDISH RYE BREAD

*This is a simple old-fashioned loaf. The original recipe started somewhere in the Midwest and is the kind of bread that is passed down from one generation to the next. Each family has a slightly different version. This recipe makes 2 loaves, and they freeze very well. A clay pan does a wonderful job.*

1 pkg. active dry yeast
1/2 cup light brown sugar, firmly packed
1/4 cup warm water (about 110°)
1/2 cup molasses
6 tbs. vegetable oil
1 1/2 tsp. salt
1 1/2 cups cold water
1 cup rye flour
6-7 cups flour (bread flour works very well here) plus flour for the board
1 tbs. caraway seeds (or more), optional

In a glass bowl, combine yeast, 1 tsp. brown sugar and warm water. Let stand until foamy, about 10 minutes.

In a small saucepan, combine molasses, oil, salt, remaining brown sugar and $\frac{1}{2}$ cup cold water. Cook over medium heat until mixture is hot, but not boiling. Transfer to a large bowl and add rye flour. Add yeast mixture and remaining 1 cup cold water. Mix well to make a batter. Add 6 cups flour and mix to form a dough. Dough should be soft, not sticky. Add more flour to get proper consistency.

Turn dough onto a floured board. Add caraway seeds, if desired. Knead until dough is smooth and elastic, 8 to 10 minutes. Transfer dough to a well-greased bowl. Cover and let rise, in a draft-free place, until dough has doubled in bulk, $2\frac{1}{2}$ to 3 hours. Punch dough down.

Divide dough in half. Place each half in a greased 9-x-5-inch loaf pan. Cover loosely and let rise until doubled in bulk, about 1 hour.

When dough has almost doubled, heat oven to 350°. When dough has doubled, bake for 50 to 60 minutes, until brown. Bread should sound hollow when tapped on the bottom. Invert onto a rack and let cool completely.

# HONEY WHOLE WHEAT BREAD

*If you own a clay loaf pan, use it for this recipe. It makes a gorgeous crust.*

1¾ cups flour
1¼ cups whole wheat flour
1½ tsp. salt
1 pkg. active dry yeast

1¼ cups warm water (about 110°)
2 tbs. honey
2 tbs. unsalted butter, softened
additional butter for topping, optional

Combine flours and salt and mix well. In a large warm bowl, sprinkle yeast over water. Let stand 5 minutes. Add honey, butter and ½ flour mixture. Beat at medium speed for 2 minutes or mix vigorously with a wooden spoon, about 300 strokes, scraping bottom and sides of bowl frequently. Add remaining flour and blend with a wooden spoon until smooth. Cover and let rise in a warm draft-free place until double in bulk, about 45 minutes.

Stir batter down with a wooden spoon and beat about 25 strokes. Turn into a generously greased 9-x-5-inch loaf pan. Smooth top of loaf, leaving a slight depression in the center. Cover and let rise in a warm place until dough reaches top of pan, about 45 minutes. Meanwhile preheat oven to 375°.

Bake until bread is well browned, about 40 to 50 minutes. Remove from oven and brush bread with additional butter if desired. Cool on a rack before slicing.

# FRUITED FRENCH TOAST SURPRISE

*This recipe evolved from my desire to use up bits and pieces of leftover bread. Any kind works; mixing them works better. Most kinds of fruit — blueberries, sliced bananas, strawberries, diced peaches, applesauce — alone or a mixture, are a real treat. This loaf can be prepared the night before and baked just before serving.*

1 loaf day-old bread, about 1 lb.
   (Italian, French, whole grain), slices
   ½-inch thick
about 2 cups fruit, your choice
4 eggs, beaten
2 cups milk (or use part half-and-half)

1 tsp. vanilla extract
3 tbs. sugar
1 tsp. cinnamon
1 tsp. nutmeg
½ tsp. salt
maple syrup, optional

Thickly butter two 9-x-5-inch glass loaf pans. Layer bread and fruit, filling all spaces with bits of bread. Top with most attractive bread slices. Combine eggs with remaining ingredients, except syrup, and pour over top of loaf, leaving about ¼-inch space (for expansion). Tap pan on the counter so egg mixture penetrates. Refrigerate overnight or let stand for at least 1 hour or more (more is better). When ready to bake, preheat oven to 350°. Bake until loaf is brown and puffy, crisp on top, and all liquid has been absorbed, about 40 minutes. Serve with or without maple syrup.

# DESSERT LOAVES

# RUM CHOCOLATE MOUSSE

*Even if you think you have the best recipe for chocolate mousse, try this one. It takes no time to prepare in a blender or food processor. Make plenty, since everyone always finds room for a second helping. If you are doubling, make the recipe twice. Most processors don't take large quantities of liquid. You can serve it with additional whipped cream, but it really isn't necessary.*

¼ cup very cold milk
1 pkg. unflavored gelatin
¾ cup boiling milk
6 tbs. dark rum (or less)
1 egg

1 tsp. vanilla extract
1 pinch salt
6 oz. semisweet chocolate chips
1 cup heavy cream
2 ice cubes

Place cold milk in a blender or food processor bowl. Add gelatin and blend for 30 seconds. Add boiling milk and blend for another 30 seconds, or until gelatin is completely dissolved. Add remaining ingredients, except ice cubes, and blend for about 1 minute. Add ice cubes and blend until they melt and the mixture is very smooth. Pour into a glass loaf pan and chill for several hours. If you are running late, you can speed up the chilling process by placing the loaf pan in the freezer for ½ hour (no more).

# WINTER CITRUS TERRINE

*This is a beautiful fruit terrine, just perfect for a winter brunch or a buffet. This cannot be a last-minute decision; the terrine needs several hours (or overnight) to jell. It is important to remove all the bitter white membrane surrounding the fruit under the rind. Don't be tempted to add fresh pineapple to any mold containing gelatin — it won't jell.*

8 large navel oranges
3 large pink grapefruits
3 large tangerines
½ cup frozen unsweetened whole raspberries or strawberries (or more), unthawed
additional fresh unsweetened citrus juice (orange, grapefruit)
⅓ cup sugar
2 tbs. unflavored gelatin
½ cup orange-flavored liqueur (Grand Marnier or Triple Sec)

Line a 9-x-5-inch nonstick loaf pan with plastic wrap, so that the wrap overhangs the pan about 3 inches on all sides. With a sharp paring knife, peel and remove all white membrane, or pith, from citrus fruit, reserving any juice. Separate fruit into segments and discard any pits. You should have about 8 cups of fruit. Combine with frozen raspberries or strawberries. Add reserved juice to unsweetened citrus juice. Pour juice into a saucepan with a large surface area and add sugar. Stir gelatin into liqueur. Set aside. Bring juices to a boil and cook over medium heat until reduced by 1/3, about 10 minutes. Whisk in softened gelatin, stirring until dissolved. Cool for a few minutes.

Combine juice mixture and fruit. Transfer to prepared loaf pan. Fold overhanging plastic over the top. Place in the freezer for 1 to 2 hours, to start the jelling process, and remove to the refrigerator. The mixture should be very cold, but not frozen. If it is getting close to serving time and the mixture has not completely set up, you can put it back in the freezer for another half hour.

Unmold the terrine by running a knife around the edges of the loaf pan. Pull on the plastic and invert the terrine onto a serving platter. Cut into slices.

# FROZEN LEMON DESSERT

*This old-fashioned dessert will please everyone. The fresh berries on top make it more special.*

¾ cup crushed vanilla wafers
3 eggs, separated
¼ cup fresh lemon juice
2 tsp. grated fresh lemon peel
¼ tsp. salt

½ cup sugar
2 tsp. cornstarch
1 cup heavy cream, whipped
fresh strawberries or raspberries for
    garnish

Press ½ of the crushed wafers into a 9-x-5-inch loaf pan. In a small bowl, beat egg yolks lightly. Place 2 cups of water in the bottom of a double boiler. Bring water to a simmer. Place egg yolks, lemon juice, lemon peel, salt, sugar and cornstarch in top of double boiler and set over simmering water. Cook for about 6 to 8 minutes, stirring constantly until custard is thick. This has to be watched or it will curdle. Pour into a large bowl. Let cool.

In a medium bowl, beat egg whites to a soft peak. Fold egg whites into custard mixture. Fold in whipped cream. Pour mixture over crushed wafers. Cover with remaining crushed wafers. Cover with plastic wrap and freeze until firm, about 2 hours, if possible. Remove pan from freezer and invert onto a platter. Decorate with berries.

# RASPBERRY ICE CREAM LOAF

*A perfect summer dessert. The key to success is delicious berries. Substitute fresh strawberries for raspberries. If you do, use strawberry gelatin instead of raspberry.*

## CRUST
¾ cup crushed graham cracker crumbs     2 tbs. sugar
½ cup butter, melted

Preheat oven to 350°. In a small bowl, combine graham cracker crumbs, butter and sugar. Mix well. Press evenly on the bottom and slightly up the sides of a 9-x-5-inch glass loaf pan. Bake for about 8 minutes until crust is set. Do not let it get too brown. Let crust cool completely before filling.

## FILLING
1 pkg. (3 oz.) raspberry-flavored gelatin     1 cup fresh raspberries (or more)
1 cup boiling water                          additional raspberries for garnish
1 pt. vanilla ice cream

In a large bowl, combine gelatin with boiling water, and stir until gelatin has completely dissolved, about 2 minutes. Add ice cream and stir until ice cream has melted and mixture is smooth. Refrigerate until mixture thickens, but is still pourable, about 20 minutes. Spread berries over cooled crust. Pour filling over berries. Refrigerate until filling has set, about 2 hours. Top with additional berries, if desired.

# EGGNOG RAISIN BREAD PUDDING

*This is holiday fare, great for a special brunch. The pudding can be baked and refrigerated for several days. To reheat, loosely cover with aluminum foil, making a few slits in the top. Place in a 350° oven for about 15 minutes.*

3 eggs
1 egg yolk
¾ cup sugar
¼ cup unsalted butter, melted
2 cups whole milk (can use part or all half-and-half)
3 tbs. brandy

2 tbs. vanilla extract
¾ tsp. nutmeg (prefer freshly grated)
¼ tsp. salt
8 slices day-old cinnamon raisin bread, torn into large pieces
*Cranberry Maple Syrup*, follows

Preheat oven to 350°. Generously butter a glass 9-x-5-inch loaf pan. Place rack in center of oven. Whisk eggs, egg yolk and sugar until light. Combine with all other ingredients, except bread and syrup. Blend well. Place bread in prepared loaf pan. Pour egg mixture on top, pressing bread into custard. Let stand for 1 hour to absorb liquid. Place loaf pan into a larger baking pan and place on middle oven rack. Pour boiling water into larger pan, to come halfway up sides of loaf pan. Bake until custard is set in the center, about 1 hour. Remove from water bath. Serve warm or at room temperature with *Cranberry Maple Syrup*.

## CRANBERRY MAPLE SYRUP

⅓ cup maple syrup
2 tbs. sugar
1 cup fresh or frozen cranberries (do not defrost)
3 tbs. unsalted butter, cut into 3 pieces
2 tbs. bourbon

In a stainless or glass pan, bring maple syrup and sugar to a boil and cook over low heat for 3 minutes. Add cranberries and cook until they pop, about 5 minutes. Remove from heat. Add butter, one piece at a time, incorporating each piece with a spoon before adding another. Add bourbon and mix well.
Serve sauce immediately with pudding or cover and refrigerate. To reheat, warm gently, adding a little water to thin, if necessary.

# APPLE STREUSEL BREAD PUDDING

*This takes just a few minutes to prepare. It is a reduced-fat recipe, enhanced by chunky applesauce. It is great for a Sunday morning brunch.*

4 cups cubed day-old good-quality French bread, 1-inch cubes
1 cup chunky applesauce (prefer homemade)
¼ cup raisins
1 tsp. cinnamon
½ tsp. nutmeg
2 eggs, lightly beaten
2 cups milk (can use 2%)
⅓ cup sugar
½ tsp. vanilla extract

**TOPPING**
¼ cup flour
¼ cup brown sugar
2 tbs. butter, chilled

Preheat oven to 350°. Butter a nonstick 9-x-5-inch loaf pan. Place 3 cups of the bread cubes in prepared loaf pan. Combine applesauce, raisins, ½ tsp. of the cinnamon, and nutmeg. Spoon evenly over bread cubes. Top with remaining bread cubes. In a medium bowl, combine eggs with milk, sugar, vanilla and remaining ½ tsp. cinnamon. Blend well. Pour over bread cubes and let stand for about 10 minutes.

Prepare topping: In a small bowl, combine flour and sugar. With a fork or pastry blender, cut in butter, until mixture is crumbly. Sprinkle over top of bread cube mixture.

Bake for 50 to 60 minutes, until a toothpick inserted into the center comes out clean. Let stand for 10 minutes before serving.

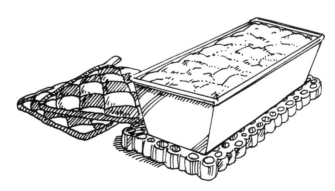

# FRUITED BREAD PUDDING

*Challah (Jewish egg bread) or any other egg bread works very well. Any fresh fruit (pears, peaches, bananas) can be substituted for the apples.*

4 cups cubed day-old egg bread,
    crusts removed if desired
4 eggs
1 egg yolk
⅔ cup sugar
3 cups milk
½ tsp. cinnamon (or more)
½ tsp. nutmeg
2 tsp. vanilla extract
1 tbs. butter
1½ cups coarsely chopped peeled apples
1 tbs. sugar (or more)
½ cup raisins or dried currants

Preheat oven to 375°. Generously butter a 9-x-5-inch loaf pan. Place rack in center of oven. Let bread cubes stand at room temperature or in a 175° oven for 1 hour to dry out slightly. In a large bowl, whisk together eggs, egg yolk, sugar and milk. Add cinnamon, nutmeg and vanilla.

Heat butter in a large skillet. Add apples and 1 tbs. sugar and sauté until apples begin to brown, about 4 minutes. Remove from heat. Add apples to egg mixture with raisins and bread cubes. Mix gently; do not break bread cubes. Place loaf pan in a larger baking pan. Add hot water to come halfway up sides of loaf pan. Bake until pudding is just set in the center, about 1 hour. Do not overbake. Remove to a wire rack and cool until lukewarm. Refrigerate for about 2 hours.

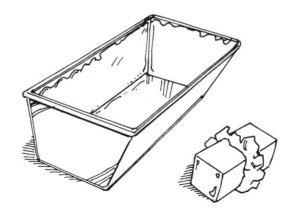

# CARROT PUDDING

*This low-calorie, sweet carrot loaf makes a nutritious dessert.*

2 eggs, room temperature, separated
2½ cups coarsely grated carrots
1 cup flour
1½ tsp. baking powder
⅔ cup sugar
2 tbs. orange juice
1 tsp. cinnamon
½ tsp. salt
½ cup raisins
2 tsp. grated orange peel, optional

Preheat oven to 350°. Generously butter a loaf pan. Beat egg yolks for 1 minute. Combine with all other ingredients, except egg whites. Beat egg whites to stiff peaks. Gently fold into carrot mixture. Spoon into prepared pan. Bake for 50 minutes or until pudding pulls away from sides of pan. Serve cold or at room temperature.

# RASPBERRY RIPPLE STREUSEL COFFEE CAKE

*This simple coffee cake works just as well (or better) with strawberry jam. Use a good-quality jam; homemade is best.*

⅔ cup butter or margarine, softened
⅔ cup sugar
2 cups flour
2 eggs, lightly beaten
2 tsp. baking powder
½ tsp. baking soda

½ tsp. salt
¾ tsp. cinnamon
½ tsp. nutmeg
⅔ cup buttermilk or plain low fat yogurt
⅓ cup raspberry jam

Preheat oven to 350°. Butter a glass loaf pan. In a large bowl, beat butter and sugar until light and fluffy. Add ¾ cup of the flour and mix just until mixture forms coarse crumbs. Remove ⅔ cup of the mixture and set aside.

Add eggs, baking powder, baking soda, salt, cinnamon and nutmeg to remaining butter-sugar mixture in bowl. Beat until smooth. Add remaining 1¼ cups flour, ½ cup at a time, alternating with buttermilk, beating until smooth after each addition. Spread batter in prepared loaf pan. Drop jam by teaspoonfuls onto batter. Using a broad blade knife or icing spatula, pull knife through batter to give marbled effect. Sprinkle reserved crumbs on top. Bake until a toothpick inserted into the center comes out clean, 30 to 40 minutes. Serve warm.

# STRAWBERRY-ORANGE COFFEE CAKE

*This simple combination of ingredients has no right to taste so good. Fresh strawberries make it worthy of company. Recently, I made the cake and forgot to add the final topping. It didn't seem to detract from the taste.*

1 cup flour
2 tbs. sugar
1½ tsp. baking powder
½ tsp. salt
¼ cup butter, softened

1 egg, lightly beaten
⅓ cup milk
2 pkg. (10 oz. each) frozen whole strawberries (prefer unsweetened), unthawed
½ cup orange marmalade

**TOPPING, optional**
¼ cup sugar
3 tbs. flour

¼ cup butter, softened

Preheat oven to 400°. Generously grease a loaf pan; use a clay pan, if possible. Combine dry ingredients. With a pastry blender or 2 knives, cut in butter until crumbly. Add egg and milk and stir until moistened. Spread in prepared loaf pan, making a small depression in the center. Combine drained strawberries with marmalade and a little strawberry juice. Spread on top of cake.

For topping, combine ¼ cup sugar with 3 tbs. flour and cut in butter until crumbly. Sprinkle evenly on top. Bake until done, about 45 minutes.

# MOCHA RAISIN DELIGHT

*This is for people who don't consider a dessert worth eating unless it has chocolate in it.*

¾ cup butter or margarine, softened
1 cup sugar
3 eggs
1 cup sour cream or plain yogurt (or combination)
1 tsp. vanilla extract
2 cups flour

1 tsp. baking powder
½ cup raisins
½ cup chopped pecans
¾ cup chocolate chips
¼ cup instant coffee crystals
confectioners' sugar, optional

Preheat oven to 350°. Grease and flour a 9-x-5-inch loaf pan. Cream together butter and sugar. Beat in eggs, one at a time. Fold in sour cream and vanilla. Combine remaining ingredients, except confectioners' sugar. Fold into butter-egg mixture. Mix until well blended. Pour into loaf pan, making sides higher than center of loaf. Bake for 1 hour or until a toothpick inserted into the center comes out clean. Let stand for 10 minutes. Turn out onto a rack until cool. Sprinkle with confectioners' sugar, if desired.

# SEPTEMBER FRUITCAKE

*The theory goes that this fruitcake should be made in September to "age" in time for Christmas. It is said that this fruitcake can last, if tightly wrapped, for a year. It allows you to mix and match dried fruit, and has no glacé fruits at all. If you cannot find barley flour, use ordinary flour.*

¼ cup orange juice
¼ cup orange liqueur (Grand Marnier, if possible)
2 lb. (about 4 cups) dried fruit (apricots, cherries, currants, dates, figs, peaches, pears, prunes, raisins)
1 cup unsalted butter, softened
¾ cup sugar
1 tsp. vanilla extract
2 tsp. grated orange peel
5 eggs
½ cup medium-dry sherry
1½ cups all-purpose flour
½ cup barley flour
½ tsp. salt
1 cup chopped walnuts
1 cup chopped pecans

Preheat oven to 300°. Butter and flour a 9-x-5-inch loaf pan. A heavy pan works best. Mix together orange juice and orange liqueur and set aside. Pit (if needed) and cut fruits to uniform size, about the size of large raisins, and combine them. Using a large bowl and an electric mixer, beat butter until light. Beat in sugar, vanilla and orange peel. Add eggs, one at a time, beating thoroughly after each addition. Beat in sherry.

Sift all-purpose flour with barley flour and salt. Stir into cake batter. Stir in chopped fruit and nuts. Spoon into prepared loaf pan, making a slight depression in the center, and bake until a toothpick inserted into the center comes out clean, about 1½ hours. Cool in pan on a rack for a few minutes. Prick top of cake with a fork and spoon orange juice-orange liqueur mixture on top. Run a knife along edge of cake to loosen. Remove cake from pan. Cool thoroughly and store in an airtight container for at least 1 month before serving.

# HOLIDAY FRUITCAKE

*Have you seen the T-shirt that reads: "Friends Don't Give Friends Fruitcake"? No other cake has been so maligned, so misunderstood. But fruitcake is traditional, and it is here to stay. Rather than fight it, we should find one we like. This recipe makes 3 fruitcakes that avoid all glacéed fruits except candied cherries (which can easily be picked out). Try substituting dried apricots; it's the wrong color, but very pleasing. This fruitcake can be baked in small loaf pans (available in an upmarket kitchen-supply shop) and given as edible gifts, with the small pan as part of the gift. Clay pans or heavy commercial-quality pans turn out splendid fruitcakes.*

6 cups coarsely chopped dates (can use part dried figs)

6 cups coarsely cut walnut pieces (do not chop)

1 cup candied cherries or dried apricots, cut into quarters

½ cup flour

6 eggs, room temperature, separated

¾ cup sugar

¾ cup dark brown sugar, firmly packed

6 tbs. unsalted butter, melted

¼ cup heavy cream or half-and-half

2 tbs. vanilla extract

1 tsp. almond extract

2 tbs. grated fresh orange peel

1 tbs. grated fresh lemon peel

1 tsp. salt

1 tbs. cinnamon

2 tsp. nutmeg

1 tsp. ground allspice

½ tsp. ground cloves

1½ cups flour (prefer whole wheat for a denser loaf)

2½ tsp. baking powder

Preheat oven to 325°. Generously butter three 9-x-5-inch loaf pans or about 10 small loaf pans. Combine dried fruit and nuts. Toss with ½ cup flour to coat (this helps distribute fruit evenly). Separate fruit with your fingers, if necessary.

Combine egg yolks and sugars in a large bowl; beat until light and fluffy. Beat in butter, cream, vanilla and almond extracts, orange and lemon peels, salt and spices. Combine whole wheat flour and baking powder; stir into egg mixture. Mix thoroughly with a wooden spoon. Stir in coated fruit.

In another large bowl, beat egg whites just until stiff peaks form. Gently fold in ¼ of the egg whites to lighten batter; fold in remaining egg whites. Do not overmix. Divide evenly and spoon into prepared pans, leaving a slight depression in the middle.

Cover pans with buttered parchment paper or aluminum foil and bake for 40 minutes (25 for small loaf pans). Continue baking until centers are firm and a toothpick inserted into the center comes out clean, about 15 to 20 minutes longer. Cool cakes in pans on wire racks. Remove from pans.

These cakes can be eaten the next day or stored for a week or more, wrapped tightly in aluminum foil. They can be frozen for several weeks, but after that, they begin to lose flavor.

# FRUITED CARROT CAKE

*This recipe makes 2 moist irresistible loaves. I used to top it with a butter-cream cheese frosting, but it is unnecessary. This is a great addition to a dessert table. It keeps in the refrigerator for a week.*

1½ cups sugar
1 cup vegetable oil
3 eggs, lightly beaten
2½ cups flour
1 tsp. salt
2 tsp. baking soda
2 tsp. cinnamon
3 cups grated carrots
1 cup coarsely chopped walnuts
1 cup raisins
1 can (6 oz.) unsweetened crushed pineapple, mostly drained

Preheat oven to 350°. Generously grease two 8-x-4-inch glass loaf pans. Mix together sugar, oil and eggs. Add all other ingredients and mix well. Pour into prepared pans. Bake for 50 to 60 minutes or until a toothpick inserted into the center comes out clean.

# SPICE LOAF CAKE

*This simple-to-make dessert is a real winner. A topping is unnecessary unless you feel that a little ice cream on top improves everything.*

1 cup chopped pecans or walnuts
2 cups flour
3/4 cup sugar
1 tbs. baking powder
1/2 tsp. baking soda
1 tsp. salt
1 tsp. cinnamon

1/2 tsp. nutmeg
1/2 tsp. allspice
1/4 tsp. ground cloves
1 cup crushed pineapple
1 egg, lightly beaten
2 tbs. vegetable oil
1 tbs. grated fresh lemon peel

Preheat oven to 350°. Oil a 9-x-5-inch loaf pan. Toast nuts in a microwave for a few minutes to enhance flavor. Sift dry ingredients into a large bowl. Stir in nuts. Combine pineapple, egg, oil and lemon peel. Add to dry ingredients and blend. Pour mixture into prepared pan and bake for 50 minutes or until a toothpick inserted into the center comes out clean. Cool on rack.

# FRENCH LEMON-YOGURT GATEAU

*"Gateau" is the French word for "cake." This is the simplest dessert to prepare, but it cannot be a last-minute decision since it must mature for a day. It keeps well.*

1 container (8 oz.) plain low fat yogurt
1¼ cups sugar
2 cups flour
1 tsp. baking powder
½ tsp. baking soda
½ tsp. salt
¾ cup vegetable oil
3 eggs, lightly beaten
grated peel of 1 lemon
juice of 1 large lemon

Preheat oven to 350°. Lightly oil a glass 9-x-5-inch loaf pan. Combine all ingredients except lemon juice. Mix with a wooden spoon until well blended. Mixture will be soft. Spoon into prepared loaf pan and bake for 1 hour and 10 minutes, until a toothpick inserted into the center comes out clean. Place on a rack and immediately pour lemon juice all over hot cake. Cover and mature for 1 day.

# CHOCOLATE CINNAMON CAKE

*This simple cake makes an outstanding dessert. You can serve it with a whipped cream or ice cream topping, but it really isn't necessary.*

1 cup flour
1 cup brown sugar, firmly packed
3 tbs. unsweetened cocoa
1 tsp. baking soda
1 tsp. cinnamon
¾ cup milk
⅓ cup butter or margarine, softened
2 tsp. white vinegar
1 tsp. vanilla extract
1 egg

Preheat oven to 350°. Lightly grease a 9-x-5-inch nonstick loaf pan. In a large bowl, combine all ingredients. Using an electric mixer, beat on low speed until moistened; beat 2 minutes longer on medium speed. Pour into prepared loaf pan. Bake for about 40 to 45 minutes, until a toothpick inserted into the center comes out clean. Cool on a rack. Serve cake warm with topping, if desired.

# BLUEBERRY CORNMEAL LOAF CAKE

*This cake is one of the pleasures of summer. Use only fresh blueberries. Serve it as is or toasted with a little vanilla ice cream as a topping. It can keep for a few days in the refrigerator.*

1½ cups flour
⅓ cup cornmeal
1½ tsp. baking powder
½ tsp. salt
½ cup plus 1 tbs. plain low fat yogurt
1 tbs. fresh lemon juice
6 tbs. unsalted butter, softened
¾ cup sugar
1 tsp. grated fresh lemon peel
2 eggs
¾ cup fresh blueberries, washed and dried
cinnamon and sugar for sprinkling

Preheat oven to 350°. Butter 8-x-4-inch glass loaf pan. Place rack in center of oven. In a bowl, combine flour, cornmeal, baking powder and salt.

Combine yogurt and lemon juice. In a large bowl, with an electric beater at medium speed, cream butter, sugar and lemon peel until light and fluffy. Beat in eggs, one at a time, beating well after each addition. Remove about 2 tbs. of dry mixture into a small bowl; toss with blueberries. At very low speed, beat remainder of dry ingredients into butter-egg mixture alternately with yogurt-lemon mixture, until just blended. Do not overmix. After batter has been mixed, gently fold in blueberry mixture. You want the blueberries to stay intact as much as possible. Spoon batter into loaf pan. Sprinkle with cinnamon and sugar. Bake for about 25 minutes. Cover loosely with aluminum foil to prevent overbrowning and bake until cake is golden and a toothpick inserted into the center comes out clean (about 35 minutes longer). Cool on a wire rack. Wrap and store overnight in pan. Serve the next day.

# APPLESAUCE RAISIN NUT CAKE

*There is no fat in this recipe, with the exception of the nuts. Cut the amount to ½ cup if you are watching fat content. This moist, spicy loaf keeps well in the refrigerator or freezer.*

2 cups flour
1½ tsp. baking soda
½ cup white sugar
½ cup light brown sugar, firmly packed
1 pinch salt
1 tsp. cinnamon
¼ tsp. ground cloves

½ tsp. nutmeg
1 egg
1 tsp. vanilla extract
grated peel of 1 orange and 1 lemon
1½ cups applesauce (prefer homemade)
1 cup coarsely chopped pecans or walnuts
½ cup raisins

Preheat oven to 350°. Lightly grease a nonstick loaf pan. Mix together flour, baking soda, sugars, salt and spices. In another bowl, beat egg lightly; add vanilla, grated orange and lemon peels and applesauce.

Combine with flour mixture and mix thoroughly but quickly. Fold in nuts and raisins. Transfer to prepared pan and bake on middle rack of oven for about 1 hour, or until a toothpick inserted into the center comes out clean. Place loaf pan on a rack and cool thoroughly in pan.

# INDEX

# SERVE CREATIVE, EASY, NUTRITIOUS MEALS WITH Nitty Gritty® COOKBOOKS

Sautés
Cooking in Porcelain
Appetizers
Recipes for the Loaf Pan
Casseroles
The Best Bagels are made at home*
  (*perfect for your bread machine)
The Toaster Oven Cookbook
Skewer Cooking on the Grill
Creative Mexican Cooking
Extra-Special Crockery Pot Recipes
Cooking in Clay
Marinades
Deep Fried Indulgences
Cooking with Parchment Paper
The Garlic Cookbook
Flatbreads From Around the World
From Your Ice Cream Maker
Favorite Cookie Recipes
Cappuccino/Espresso: The Book of
  Beverages
Indoor Grilling

Slow Cooking
The Best Pizza is made at home*
  (*perfect for your bread machine)
The Well Dressed Potato
Convection Oven Cookery
The Steamer Cookbook
The Pasta Machine Cookbook
The Versatile Rice Cooker
The Dehydrator Cookbook
The Bread Machine Cookbook
The Bread Machine Cookbook II
The Bread Machine Cookbook III
The Bread Machine Cookbook IV:
  *Whole Grains and Natural Sugars*
The Bread Machine Cookbook V:
  *Favorite Recipes from 100 Kitchens*
The Bread Machine Cookbook VI:
  *Hand-Shaped Breads from the
  Dough Cycle*
Worldwide Sourdoughs From Your
  Bread Machine
Recipes for the Pressure Cooker

The New Blender Book
The Sandwich Maker Cookbook
Waffles
The Coffee Book
The Juicer Book
The Juicer Book II
Bread Baking (traditional)
No Salt, No Sugar, No Fat Cookbook
Cooking for 1 or 2
Quick and Easy Pasta Recipes
The 9x13 Pan Cookbook
Extra-Special Crockery Pot Recipes
Low Fat American Favorites
Now That's Italian!
Fabulous Fiber Cookery
Low Salt, Low Sugar, Low Fat Desserts
Healthy Cooking on the Run
Muffins, Nut Breads and More
The Wok
New Ways to Enjoy Chicken
Favorite Seafood Recipes
New International Fondue Cookbook

**For a free catalog, write or call:**
**Bristol Publishing Enterprises, Inc.**
**P.O. Box 1737**
**San Leandro, CA 94577**
**(800) 346-4889; in California, (510) 895-4461**